A NEW ROAD TO ANCIENT TRUTH

Tenko San and his wife going for Takuhatsu

A NEW ROAD
TO
ANCIENT TRUTH

by

ITTOEN TENKO-SAN

Being extracts from his writings translated by
Makoto Ohashi in collaboration with
Marie Beuzeville Byles
with an introduction by
MARIE BEUZEVILLE BYLES

London
GEORGE ALLEN & UNWIN LTD
RUSKIN HOUSE MUSEUM STREET

PRINTED IN GREAT BRITAIN
in 11 on 12 point Juliana type
BY THE BLACKFRIARS PRESS LTD
LEICESTER

AUTHOR'S FOREWORD

———————

In having nothing lies inexhaustible wealth
                    TENKO NISHIDA

CONTENTS

Contents

ILLUSTRATIONS

INTRODUCING ITTOEN

It was by chance that I came to Ittoen, the Garden of the one Light, a peaceful happy community of something under 300 men, women and children on the outskirts of Kyoto the ancient capital of Japan. (But of course nothing happens by chance; all is the result of the working of laws of nature whose operation our own thoughts and aspirations help to shape.) I had come to Japan to see something of Zen in the country where it is chiefly practised. It was a Zen priest who mentioned Ittoen, but it was because of the courtesy and efficiency of the girl at the enquiry desk of the Kyoto hotel that I was at length able to arrange a visit.

Two acquaintances came with me. We drove through the narrow streets of Yamashina, crossed an avenue of cherry trees and a swiftly flowing stream, and entered the little village of Kosenrin, the outward sign that Ittoen has its roots in a practical economy as well as in the invisible life of the spirit.

Here we were greeted by the teacher of English and a former Baptist minister who also spoke English. The teacher, a little woman of thirty-six, was the Toban in charge of foreign guests. They led us through the village which lies under the high hills which surround Yamashina. A sparkling brook flows down from steep forests starred with wild pink azaleas. It winds between small buildings, maple trees and pines and soft moss lawns with yellow irises. Sometimes it widens into lakelets where goldfish sport among reflections of stone bridges and ornamental stone lanterns. In the village is a school, knitting school, printing works, agricultural research bureau, and large cook-house, which provides food for the

15

whole community. Outside the village are bamboo groves, vegetable gardens, fruit trees and cultivated forests.

Finally our guides took us to the visitors' reception room at the entrance of which we removed our shoes and were given the type of sandal usually provided at sight-seeing temples. The room was furnished European style, so that we sat, not on cushions on the floor, but on upholstered chairs! There was a picture of Bodhidharma, the Chinese founder of Zen, and a photograph of Rajendra Prasad, the disciple of Gandhi and first President of India.

We were told we were now to meet Tenko Nishida San, affectionately known as Tenko-San, the Founder of Ittoen over sixty years before. (San is a suffix of respect like Mr, Mrs or Miss. It is hyphenated on the title pages to prevent indexing under 'San' instead of 'Tenko'!) When he came into the room I was frankly disappointed. He seemed not to belong to this world. But one of my companions spontaneously held her hands prayerwise and said, 'To think that you are the Founder of all this!' He was over ninety years old and a little deaf but otherwise in possession of his faculties and still the head of the community. But as far as I was concerned I was unable to make contact with him. This was not because of my suspicions of gurus acquired when in India, for I did not then know that many thousands account him not merely a guru, but a wholly enlightened One comparable to Buddha or Christ. It was not until he smiled when he bade us farewell that I realized there might be something out of the ordinary about him.

Even on the second and third visits[1] when I stayed for some days I was still not moved by him. Indeed I remember feeling slightly frustrated because he insisted on showing me round when I felt I ought to take advantage of the sunshine for photography. What impressed me on the second visit was the extraordinary atmosphere of peace. After that second visit I found my life strangely reorientated. It was not, however, until I visited Japan two and a half years later that I heard

[1] For an account of these visits see my *Paths to Inner Calm.*

what an amazing life Tenko San's had been and the enormous influence he had exercised. His mind and body were now sinking down to earthly decay, and I was a little sad that the law of karma could not vouchsafe to me the privilege of knowing this modern spiritual genius when I first went to the East in 1953, while he was still at the height of his powers physically and mentally as well as spiritually.

When the idea came to ask Makoto Ohashi, a member of Ittoen, to write something about Ittoen, I did not envisage his translating Tenko San's own words. That was his idea entirely. But when I began to read what he translated, Tenko San spoke directly to my heart and I knew that he would speak to the hearts of others also. It is not that he has discovered a new Truth. The Upanishads, Buddha, Laotsu, Christ, Ramakrishna, Ramana Maharshi, Mahatma Gandhi and many others have found the same Truth, which of course ceases to be Truth as soon as it is put into words—that is why, say Easterners, Westerners can hardly ever find enlightenment! Be that as it may, Tenko San has thrown the new light of present experience and actual life here and now upon that old Truth. And more important still, he has discovered a new road to it— that is if any thing can be called new when there is no new thing under the sun.

This ancient Truth—which ceases to be true as soon as I try to explain it!—is that Light, as Tenko San calls it, or God or Nirvana—alone is. It is the One Living Reality. All else is empty of reality. If we live in complete and unquestioning dependence on Light, all is well.

There is Power within the universe to deliver man from suffering, and this deliverance includes provision for his material as well as spiritual needs. But this Power cannot operate except in so far as we surrender ourselves to guidance of Light and live in accord with it.

A living manifestation of this great Reality is shown in the following description of the ideal man, one of the earliest and most treasured of Tenko San's writings. Ittoen's life has altered outwardly very considerably since it was written, but it is still chanted at every morning worship and is still regarded as expressing the basic reality upon which life rests.

A LIVING MANIFESTATION OF THE ONE REALITY
(ICHI-JIJITSUI)

A man is standing at the roadside. Although he is an ordinary man he seems to be illumined by Light. At times he holds his hands prayerwise as if worshipping the Invisible. At other times he enters homes to straighten the footwear at the door, sweep the garden, clean the toilet, or tidy the storeroom.

If he is hungry he stands near the kitchen his hands prayerwise. If he feels that the giver's heart is not sincere he does not accept what is offered. When he does accept he meditates momentarily and the giver's heart is purified. Unless he cannot avoid it he never accepts food better than is given to a servant, nor takes a seat nor accepts any favoured treatment. When people want him to do so he stays in their homes and does whatever work may be asked of him. In these homes he treats all with equal respect and gratitude and works diligently and with gratitude for the blessings received. Although he has a family of his own its members are not unduly attached to one another and each enjoys this life of service with perfect ease.

Being neither priest nor layman, he has limitless resources of Fukuden,[1] but he is also a labourer. He is nurtured by Light and does not work in order to live but to express gratitude for the blessings he has received.

Rich men whose riches are the source of worry come to this truth seeker for help, and even before he has spoken they find the cause of their worries. Poor men bewailing their poverty also come to this truth seeker for help. They

[1] Purified wealth—see Glossary.

learn what riches they possess, how to be thankful for the blessings they have received, and because of their gratitude to find joy in living.

The power of civilizations has no meaning for this truth seeker. Civilizations are built up by men and by men they are destroyed. These men sorrow for what they lack and suffer for what they have.

Even as the pleasures of this world seem hollow to this truth seeker, so too do the pleasures of the heaven worlds. When asked about life and death he smiles but does not answer. When asked who he is he holds his hands prayer-wise and then turns to sweep the dust from the road. When one who believes in him asks him the way to truth, he answers that he is ashamed because of his lack of virtue. When pressed for a fuller answer he replies that he is led by Light[1] and walks and acts in accord with the Formless Form.

He does not believe exclusively in either God or Buddha or Confucius but regards all these as within the gate of Funi-No-Komyo or the Light of Oneness. Anguish, sorrow, want and trouble, even the cause of the rise and fall of nations and the way to the rebuilding of the world—all these seem clear to him, just as the sound of a bell is clear when it is struck or things become clear when a light shines upon them. If praised or admired for his wisdom, he says that it is that of Funi-No-Komyo, Light of Oneness, and that it is this which lights his work.

Gentle, modest and diligent, he has no desire to compete with others, neither has he desire for possessions though he delights in producing plenitude. He neither affirms nor denies any of the world's ideologies, but with innocent heart trusts all things to the operation of natural law.

A mortal man? The Light Itself? Or maybe an idiot. He himself does not know. How much less do others! Never-

[1] Light (or God) is that which cannot be described except by negatives such as infinite, uncreated, formless. M.B.B.

theless here is a living manifestation of the One Reality.

*　　　　*　　　　*

Could this homeless one, dependent on Light alone and giving menial service with selfless humility and without payment, exist in our affluent modern societies with their labour-saving devices, no spare sleeping accommodation, whose inmates are usually all out during the day and looking at TV in the evenings?

That such could and do exist is shown by the anonymous 'Peace Pilgrim' who tramps through America delivering her message of peace, and who owns nothing and lacks for nothing. And it should be remembered that Japan like America has none of the wandering 'holy men' or sadhus of India.

It would seem that this homeless one could exist just as well in any modern Western country as in Japan, provided of course that he really did depend upon Light alone, and truly wished to make himself lower than the lowest and give humble service. Nearly all the world's spiritual geniuses have been homeless and propertyless and perhaps the only remedy for our worry riddled Western societies would be the example of a few like Tenko San's early disciples.

'But you yourself', asks a candid friend, 'what are you yourself doing to provide this example? Have you not a reasonable income? Do you not own a pleasant little house?' The candid friend is perfectly right. I can only hope that in the next incarnation—if such exist—I may be able to follow Tenko San a little more effectively. One would enjoy marvellous freedom if one had no possessions. I caught a glimpse of what this would mean when many years ago I suddenly realized that making money and being successful did not matter. It was as if a burden had been lifted from my back.

But even though we cannot hope to know the freedom that Tenko San knew, we can all learn to do the work that falls to our hands without regard for payment or non-payment, thanks or blame, but solely as an opportunity for service. I can vouch that this attitude makes all work a joy, and that compassion arises without effort when one is not concerned whether one gets anything either material or emotional or mental in return for the work.

The candid friend having been graciously thus dismissed now raises a further objection to this ideal man really being the ideal. The objection is that by spending his time sweeping floors he is not making use of the talents with which nature has endowed him. We shall see from the stories which follow that this is by no means the case. Although all Ittoen's members start with menial work and continue to do it, nonetheless when the time is ripe the opportunity always arises for them to use their special talents. The artist was asked to sculpture statues, the mathematician to teach mathematics and the natural masseur to exercise his gift.

There is however a far graver objection to this ideal man being the ideal for our Western societies, where by and large people know nothing of enlightenment or dying to self, or surrender to Light (or God). We of the West tend to be satisfied that doing good is itself a virtue and that by thinking things out with our intellects we can arrive at truth. So certain are we that doing good is all that is required that it has been said you can often recognize the people to whom the good things are done by the hunted look on their faces! For example there is the hostess whose guest (perhaps thinking of Tenko San) cleans and tidies the house, especially the toilet, so that her hostess can find nothing where it ought to be! This could easily happen if Westerners tried to follow Tenko San's teaching without understanding from experience the inner meaning, the dying to self, and moving with Formless Light or Formless Form, to do which the intellect can help not one iota.

In the West we tend to suffer from activity mania as well as intellectual arrogance, and easily excuse our failure to move with Formless Light so long as we are engaged in worthy causes or writing learned theses about Formless Light. We have as a rule no inkling of the meaning of sitting still, let alone *being* still, and without this it is hardly possible to come under the direction of Formless Light.

Only a few of Ittoen's members make a practice of 'sitting straight' or 'eating time and space', as the art of meditation is sometimes called. But the quietness of morning and evening sutra chanting is taken for granted, and all that Ittoen's members do is expected to be done in a prayerful spirit. As I walked chanting sutras along the paths with the trainees who had come for a four-day training course, I could feel the spirit of dedication with which they had undertaken their work. It was not the good turns they had done that mattered, but the spirit of dedication to Light.

Further, the Easterner has inherited the art of *'being'* still, physically as well as mentally. I noticed this in India and marvelled at how the Indian mother would gather her children under her sari and settle down on the concrete railway platform for half the night. In Japan I saw hundreds of school children sitting, or more correctly kneeling, for four and a half hours on hard boards during the performance of the No plays.

For us of the West who have none of this ability to sit still and even less ability to calm our thoughts, I cannot see how we can understand, let alone follow, the path of this ideal man, unless along with menial service we consciously set aside times for cultivating the art of being still and calming our thoughts by the practice of meditation. The Easterner can perhaps afford to give up his meditation period to help a sick friend, but we cannot afford to do so unless we set aside another period instead. Without this practice our emulation of the activities of this ideal man might be embarrassing to say the least of it.

As we read the anecdotes that Tenko San tells we should constantly bear in mind this basic difference in the training and heritage of East and West. But this consideration does not lessen the ability of Tenko San's teaching to solve the prac-

tical problems that he likes to be asked about. The following
is an example of one of these. The story appeared in *Hikari*
('The Light') in 1926.

'This is an account of how Mr S. found the new way of life.
I was travelling by invitation on a lecture tour in Manchuria
when I came to the town of Eiko. After a two-hour lecture at
a club there, Mr S. kindly offered a night's lodging to me and
my two travelling companions. The house was large and combined Japanese and European styles. There was an informal
discussion with several lay followers of Ittoen before everyone
departed and I was alone with Mr S. He was obviously waiting
for this and at once began to speak.

"I have got into a desperate situation. Do you mind listen-
ing to my story?"

"Certainly, please tell me."

He continued, "As you know I have been trading in bean-
curd produced in Manchuria. Due to the depression which
has now lasted several years, I have suffered terrible losses. I
am not only penniless but deeply in debt. As I read your
books I tried to picture how I could put your ideas of the new
life into operation. I told my creditors about my difficulties
and offered them all my property. This house is not mine; a
friend lent it to me without charge—business is so slack that
no one wants to rent houses as large as this these days. I have
two clerks. I can't pay them their salaries, but they have
worked faithfully for me for many years and they are not
demanding what is due to them. My wife has lost confidence
in me because I have sold all her belongings. To my shame
even the mattress and covers for your use tonight do not
belong to me . . . "

Mr S. said all this without stopping. He now wiped the
perspiration from his face and drew a deep breath. I understood why he had invited me to his house. I rejoiced at his
earnestness for I like being asked about matters of practical
concern. I do not attach much importance to theoretical ques-

tions. I was deeply interested and listened with bated breath as he continued.

"I am not only penniless, but . . . " He hesitated.

"How much are you in debt?"

"About five hundred thousand."

"Do you owe it to banks or to individuals?"

"To both."

"I suppose your creditors have forgiven you your default now that you have offered to give them all your property."

"All have forgiven me except one. But this one is adamant. I am now redoubling my efforts, but he always stands in the way of my getting on my feet again. When I told him I had literally nothing more to give, he asked me to lend him my clerk. My clerk objected and said he would never do such a ridiculous thing as consent to being lent."

Mr S. had come to a deadlock. This was no pose. Both his words and attitude were desperately serious. He was confronted with economic catastrophe. Finally he added gravely, "What should a follower of Ittoen do in such a case?"

I started to speak but he interposed.

"Can you tell me the right way?"

I was about to answer but instead I prayed in silence. Mr S. gazed at me intently as he waited for my reply.

"You are truly happy now?" I queried.

"Why?"

"Because honestly and without mental reservation you probed to the depth of the matter and put your trust in Light alone."

I waited expectantly. Mr S. attempted to speak, but somehow the words would not come. I continued, "If you should go into Ittoen and once and for all time give up yourself, you would surely be saved."

"Do you mean I would have to go to Kyoto?"

"No, not at all. You can go into Ittoen anywhere."

"But I have given up all my possessions already."

"No, there remains one thing you have not yet abandoned."

"But what could I have concealed from you? I have kept nothing secret."

"True, but there is still one thing. It is right under my very nose."

"Please tell me what it is."

He might well ask. Who would notice it? He would certainly receive a shock if I named it. But I had no alternative. I said, "It is your very body."

He suddenly tensed and could not speak.

I continued, "You should bring to your creditor this body which you have abandoned. He will be glad to have you do Takuhatsu[1] in his house in place of your clerk to whom he would have to pay wages."

Mr S. became lost in a daze. Then he sat up straight and with a somewhat reproachful face asked, "But what would become of my wife and family?"

I replied, "Even to think of such a thing is asking too much. When I earnestly try to make amends I do not use my family as an excuse for not doing so." He tried to speak but I went on relentlessly, "When one has complete faith in Light and is truly faithful to It then Light will keep the family alive."

I spoke very firmly and the conversation ended. We sat in silence for some time. Mr S. was a man of clear thought and firm determination and he seemed to have been deeply moved. Finally we each said "Goodnight" and parted.

The next evening I gave another lecture in the city and apparently some of the creditors were in the audience. Then I left the city and went to Hoten. Here I received a letter from Mr S. It is one of my most precious and revered.

In this letter he said that after beginning this new way of life he was cleaning the floor of the assembly hall of a high school one day, as if he were a coolie of the lowest class. As

[1] Takuhatsu means literally to get one's food in everyday life. In Zen Buddhism it means taking the begging bag or bowl round the village. For Tenko San it means humble menial service given without expectation of remuneration or thanks. In both cases there is the certainty that Light will provide for the one who has surrendered to it.   M.B.B.

he swept the mud from the porch he found tears streaming down his face. They were tears, not of sorrow, but of thankfulness. Two thoughts came into his mind, "How could I not have known before of the existence of such a world as this?" and, "May it please God that I be permitted to continue this way of life." These two thoughts reveal the existence of this World of Light, of which he would never have known had he not plunged into it and practised Takuhatsu.

He went on to say that it was on the day I left Eiko that he made his decision. He approached his creditor and said, "I am sorry I have grudged you my own body. Instead of my clerk to whom it would have been necessary to pay wages, I deliver up myself. You need not pay *me* for doing Takuhatsu for you." The creditor was very surprised, but as he had heard of Ittoen, he in part understood and said, "You mean the Takuhatsu of Ittoen? But what about your family? Have you thought about the effect it would have upon them?" Mr S. replied, "Tenko San scolded me when I asked him that same question. But now I know myself that if I give a thought to my family, I am not being truly faithful in seeking to repay my debt to you." The creditor was deeply moved at the unexpected turn of events and Mr S.'s sincerity. He said, "I realize what you mean and I appreciate your faithfulness. Don't worry any longer about your debt, I hope you will make a vigorous fresh start, and if you want some small financial assistance, you can look to me." Mr S. was completely taken aback, and thought to himself, "I never knew before that you were such a reasonable man." When there is pure and genuine faithfulness, everybody is moved by it. But this can never be realized by people with today's business ethics. Since then, Mr S. has lived his new life with devotion and thankfulness, his conduct gives assurance to others and fearlessness to himself. He is now doing Takuhatsu in a business office, and his family, about whom all were so anxious, is serving pleasantly in the house.'[1]

[1] It is only in the very modern business world that the house and place of business are separate.

It should be pointed out that this story was told before the depression ended. What happened afterwards is not told, nor whether Mr S. returned to business life with this new attitude of trust in Light and humble service to all. He may have done so. It is possible, but not easy, to live this new life in the business world. Raychandbhai, who was Mahatma Gandhi's early teacher, was a wealthy jeweller, and one of the Buddha's foremost disciples, Ananthapindika, the friend of the orphan and destitute, was a wealthy merchant. And when I was in Tokyo and Nagoya I met several wealthy business men, Friends of Light, as Ittoen's lay disciples are called, who were humble and applied Ittoen principles in their undertakings. These are outstanding exceptions to the general rule that it is easier for a camel to pass through the eye of a needle than for a rich man to enter the Kingdom of Heaven, or the new life of which Tenko San speaks.

*   *   *

Several readers of this manuscript have commented adversely on Mr S.'s failure to confer with his wife in his troubles, and worse still to part with her property without her permission. To understand this we must bear in mind that in Japanese family life the husband and father is the undisputed head, even now, and still more when this was written, and that his rule is absolute as in feudal days. His wife is not his companion in our sense of the term; she is his housekeeper and mother of his children. We shall see later that she is not even addressed by the usual term of respect given to all except inferiors. A remarkable thing, as we shall see later, is that Tenko San, like Christ and Buddha, cuts completely across this inferiority of women. All alike are 'fed by Light' and dependent alone upon it, therefore none is superior or inferior.

The story of Mr S. may seem far removed from life in our affluent societies where there is no coolie class, and kindly laws of bankruptcy prevent creditors from oppressing their debtors unduly. But there are others in perhaps even more

parlous states. The applicability of the laws of nature under-
lying this drama of Mr S. will unfold in various circumstances
as Tenko San tells the stories of Ittoen and the life of the
Kosenrin community, and they are expressed in the Five
Prayers that are chanted every morning in the worship at
Ittoen.

THE FIVE PRAYERS

May we be born anew into the World of the One Light
and live only as Light allows.

May we revere the Essence which is the same in all
religions and work for the goal which is also the same
for all.

May we serve others in the spirit of Penitence and in
gratitude for the gifts we have received.

May we perfect our lives by shaping them in accord
with the sacred laws of nature.

And may we thus return to our Home, and move in the
Paradise of Formless Light.

*   *   *

The community of Ittoen which seeks to live these ancient
truths, is like many other religious communities of both past
and present in that it admits of no individual property. Anything that is given to a member is offered to Light, and legally
vested in Kosenrin. Those who go outside to work bring their
wages to Light. Those who work within the community give
their services to Light. Ittoen is not unique in this. Nor is it
unique, at least in Japan, in that the outward form of its
religion is syncretic, that is to say, it embraces all religions,
for it finds the same Light at the heart of all, call it God,
Buddha or Christ, as you prefer.

Tenko San claims that Ittoen is not a religion, syncretic or
otherwise, but a way of life. Probably nearly all founders of
the great religions claimed the same. But unlike Tenko San
very few instituted a form of worship which (although pre-

dominantly Mahayana Buddhist) deliberately gathers together symbols from various faiths. In the worship hall where members meet for sutra chanting in the morning and evening, the central shrine is made from pieces of shrines of all religions. In one side shrine is inscribed the name for God the God of Shinto and all other faiths and in the other the name for Buddha. On the beam above the central shrine is a sun with twelve points of light, a Buddhist swastika made into a circle by bending its arms, and in the centre a Greek cross. A Zen inscription, memorial tablets to the departed, and a prayer that the Emperor may live for ever, complete the unified syncretic nature of this worship hall of One Light.

As Ittoen is not unique in its community of ownership, nor in its syncretic nature, nor in its insistence on humble selfless service, for which last many Catholic orders as well as the Ramakrishna Mission are noted—what then makes it unique? It is what Tenko San calls the path of Sange or Penitence, which he discovered when Light flooded into his being.

This book is a paraphrase of a translation of Tenko San's own words taken mainly from his best-known book, *The Way of Penitence*. In this he relates many colourful stories about its members which explain his discovery. As we read what Tenko San has spoken and written we begin to understand how Sange or Penitence is probably the reason for that happy peaceful atmosphere which seems to surround the visitor as soon as he crosses the bridge and enters the little village of Kosenrin under the high forested hills.

*　　　*　　　*

But now who is this Tenko Nishida San?

He was born in 1872 and was therefore over the age of ninety when I met him in 1963 and first learned about Ittoen. He came from a well-to-do business family, but his education ended with the primary school. He later felt grateful that a higher education did not lead him into the temptation of thinking he was clever, but from the internal evidence of his writings it is clear that he had educated himself far beyond the primary standard and that he could have been extraordinarily clever in business had he so chosen.

When he was little more than a youth he was in charge of a large agricultural scheme for the reclamation of waste land. This would almost certainly have proved successful had he not come up against the problem of one group, the workers, striving against another group, the financiers. He discovered the terrifying truth that society is based upon self-seeking, and realized that so long as this persists there is no hope of a peaceful society, let alone a peaceful world. He tells us how he gave up both the project and his own property. But even after he had given up 'the things of this world' and become a homeless beggar, relatives and business acquaintances still regarded his advice as worth having.

He had been married at the age of nineteen. When he gave up his property he hoped his wife would follow in his footsteps with their two sons. But she never understood the meaning of the way he had found, and she went back to her own people and a life of physical comfort.

The idea that a man may abandon his wife and children and become 'as one dead', is something that both the Japanese and Western mind find hard to understand. But the biographies of great saints and sages of all religions show most have given up personal affection and have literally 'gone forth from home to homelessness' as the Buddhist scriptures put it. The Buddha left wife and child. Christ, as far as we know, was never married, but we do know he had 'nowhere to lay his head' and that he is reported to have made such extreme statements as: 'There is no man that hath forsaken house or brethren or sisters or mother or wife or children or lands, for my sake but will receive a thousandfold now, and in the world to come, eternal life' (Mark 10), or again, 'If any man come to me and hate not his mother and father and brethren and sisters . . . he cannot be my disciple' (Luke 10). Even though the word 'hate' may have been far stronger than was actually used, it is nonetheless clear that Christ, like Tenko San, places obedience to Light above so-called family obligations. But of course neither Christ nor Tenko San declare that a man may desert his family merely because of his own desires. The condition of becoming as one dead is that he must have surrendered to Light (or God or Christ) and died to self. When he does this the laws of nature are such that what is necessary is provided. Tenko San tells how food and lodging came to him, and he is satisfied that if his wife had had the same faith, she also would have received all that was necessary. When Gandhi 'espoused the Lady Poverty' his wife followed him, as the traditional Hindu wife also follows her husband. Perhaps she did not have his sublime faith in God, but she had faith in him and that was enough. Ramakrishna was another spiritual genius who was married, but his wife was his companion and had the same faith as he. Neither lacked for material necessities.

As we read the stories of these great ones, as well as of many lesser ones, we are a little tantalized to know how their worldly needs came to be thus provided. Tenko San's writings are the first I have read which go into details of what happens when one gives up lands and money for the sake of Light, and receives in return not only unbelievable peace and happiness but material things as well. His wife preferred to keep the material things she knew. This was for her to decide. Tenko San waited ten years in the hope that she would find Light. She did not do so and in 1913 he married a member of Ittoen. Later on, his two sons by his first wife (he had none by the second) found Light and followed their father's footsteps to Ittoen. His grandson is now in charge of the community— his sons both being dead.

Of course all who find Light do not necessarily give up their possessions or family life. It may be their task to bear the difficulties these things bring in a spirit of detachment and trust in the guidance of Light. Ittoen has thousands of lay disciples.

In the year Tenko San remarried, a lay adherent gave to Ittoen its first permanent home. It was the forerunner of the present village of Kosenrin, which was the beginning of the end of the absolute homelessness of the first members. Similar religious movements usually have the same history. Their first devotees literally 'have nowhere to lay their heads', so that they are forced to be physically as well as spiritually dependent on Light, or God. Gradually they acquire lands and possessions. In the end they have a life of more security than other people because they live in a community where none seeks to grasp anything for himself.

It was probably because Tenko San saw this likely development that in 1919 he started what is known as the Rokuman Gyogan movement. This name was coined by Tenko San. 'Roku' means six, the six paths of Zen to reach the Further Shore of enlightenment, namely almsgiving, keeping the precepts, perseverance, hard training, equanimity and attainment of wisdom. 'Man' means 10,000. Tenko San aspired to visit 5 homes for toilet cleaning each day he went out, and to go out 200 days in the year, that is 1,000 per annum or 10,000 in 10 years. 'Gyogan' means a prayer. This movement meant that members of Ittoen thenceforth systematically and regularly left the shelter of the community to visit the homes of people along the roadside and asked to be permitted to clean their toilets. I have described one of these expeditions in *Paths to Inner Calm* where I have also quoted the Rokuman Gyogan Prayer which is chanted before members set out on these expeditions and also at morning worship. The following translation is somewhat improved on the earlier one.

ROKUMAN GYOGAN PRAYER

Oh Light of Heaven and Earth!
accept this humble act of service
as a means to worship Thee.
I have nothing else to offer,
for I have no virtue of my own.

I have searched for the root
of all the troubles of the whole wide world,
and I have found that it lay within my own heart.
It was from this knowledge
sprang this act of worship.

I therefore entreat
that I may serve in this manner,
and that this service may make
for the strengthening
of the moral foundations of our land.

I cling to Thee alone, Oh Light!
that protects the rocks
that lie at the foundation
of the eight provinces of our country.

May this act of mine help to fulfil
the desire of the great emperor Meiji,
who sang that all men the four seas over
are one brotherhood.

This is where we come to the new road to old truths and
the uniqueness of Tenko San's teaching.

Two years later Tenko San's first book, *Life of Sange*, or
Life of Penitence, was published and soon became a best seller.
After it had run into 301 editions and sold over 600,000
copies he deliberately withdrew it from public sale because he
did not want to start another new religion (of which over 100
are registered in Japan) whose adherents would not sincerely
try to put his teaching into practice in their daily living.

'Sange' means repentance or penitence, but as I see it there
is an overtone to the word Sange not found in the English
equivalents. If I attempt to explain this the reader must
remember that the explanation is entirely my own. The Elders
of Ittoen told me that there are many facets to Tenko San's
teaching and that one person understands one facet, and
another another. This is certainly true, and the reader must

search the chapters that follow and draw his own deductions by putting into practice the teaching as he understands it.

As I see it, the overtone of the word Sange is the need not merely to be sorry for our own wrongdoing, but to give up the sense of individual selfhood that is the source of all evil. An evangelist remarked that 'I' lies in the middle of sin. This expresses the overtone of the word Sange. The path of Sange does not mean that we sit down and weep over our short-comings or even feel remorseful, for this only accentuates our egoism. What is required is to die to self altogether. As will be seen from Tenko San's anecdotes, the major aspect of Sange is the death of selfhood and surrender to Light, or perhaps we might call it at-one-ment with all, so that we take to ourselves the evil as well as the good of all creation. If the Zen devotee feels that this has a Zen flavour he may be interested to know that for ten years after he adopted the homeless life Tenko San was on friendly terms with a Zen Roshi. But Ittoen has none of the harshness of Zen simply because of the introduction of Sange, self blame. It is a community of loving kindness where no harsh word, let alone a violent blow, breaks the harmony.

Sange is the basis of Tenko San's philosophy. In the poem quoted he tells how he searched for the cause of the evils of the whole wide world, found that it lay within his own heart and that the way to expiate these evils was humble, selfless service.

I was a little nonplussed when I first read about Sange—the need to take on my own shoulders the burden of all evils and never blame anyone else. But when I started to apply it, I found the theory worked amazingly well in practice. Obviously Tenko San did not evolve it from intellectual reasoning, but from the fact that it is a law of life. Whenever there was any feeling of tension or discord, I discovered that if I looked within myself for the fault and did not blame the other person, then tension and discord died. Furthermore the defaulter often became reformed, probably because when one takes the blame oneself a feeling of compassion arises, and this is sensed by the other. It is not a question of forgiving, but of unconsciously dropping one's previous feeling of antagonism and superiority. This occurs without effort when one looks within oneself for the fault. Further, this would seem to be the only possible way in which peace between nations as well as between opposing groups can be brought about.

Although Tenko San was for a while a member of parliament, generally speaking he stood aside with complete detachment from 'worthy causes', seeing only too clearly that without a changed heart outer reforms are not possible. But provided there is that inward changed heart, I do not think Tenko San teaches that people like Mahatma Gandhi and Martin Luther King should cease from their work of trying to right injustices and evils.

What matters is the selfless service and the shouldering of the responsibility of all evil. Christ is said to have taken upon himself the burden of the sins of all mankind. Tenko San's teaching throws a completely new light on this ancient truth.

There is a law governing human relationships, an expanding, growing law. Or, more correctly, man's understanding of this law grows and expands even as the astronomer's understanding of 'the expanding universe'. This law moves from conflict to understanding.

The natural reaction of the instinct for the preservation of the individual self is the urge to hit back. Moses insisted that the retaliation should be just—an eye for an eye, a tooth for a tooth—that is to say, you must not take a man's life when he has merely put out your eye. Some of the prophets of the Old Testament dimly perceived that there is a further law, the law of love, or more correctly, an expansion of the old law. But it was Christ who explicitly taught the existence of this law of love, a force far stronger than just retaliation. Five hundred years previously the Buddha had revealed the same law, 'not by hatreds are hatreds calmed but only by non-hatreds', and his long ministerial life of forty-five years—or forty-nine according to Japanese reckoning—was a continuous proof of the efficacy of love and compassion.

The teaching of both Christ and Buddha shows that they understood that this law of love requires 'the casting out of the beam from one's own eye' before the law of love can operate. But neither of them made any clear enunciation of this need to take the entire blame upon oneself. Gandhi went further than either, for he always looked within himself and his own people for their shortcomings before he blamed others. Ahimsa, non-violence and love were all-powerful. If, despite what he taught about this, there were, nonetheless, riots and violence, he would look within himself to find where he had failed, and very often he would fast to purify his mind.

Similarly, before blaming the British he would blame his own people. They had become downtrodden because they had been cowards. He was never filled with 'righteous indignation', that is to say, he did not ask the British to bear the whole of the blame. It is significant that even before the struggle ended, he had won the affection and respect of vast numbers of the conquering race. But even Gandhi did not expressly enunciate the necessity for taking the blame for all evils upon one's own shoulders.

This law is the inner meaning of the crucifixion. There cannot be true love unless Christ takes upon himself the sins of the world. It also explains the dark colour at the throat of the Hindu God Shiva, who, because of his infinite compassion, has drunk the poison of the evil of the world so that it no longer has power to harm. But neither story is carried to its logical and spiritual conclusion that the Saviour is not a God external to ourselves, but within our own hearts. It is the Christ spirit or the Shiva spirit within ourselves who must accept the sins of all mankind. Unless we can do this there cannot be an ending of self-righteousness and superiority, and without this ending there cannot be the fullness of love and compassion which reconciles and brings harmony.

It has been for Tenko San to discover this law and show it

as the basis of the path to peace. Without taking the blame and identifying oneself with evil as well as good, it would seem impossible for most people to find friendship for, let alone oneness with, the opponent. I say most people, for there *are* other paths. But for ordinary persons facing such daily problems as the need to forgive the children who stole the apples, or the next door neighbour who maligned one's character, I suggest that Tenko San's teaching of Sange is the easiest way of eliminating these fatal obstructions of pride, self-righteousness and superiority.

This way is applicable, not only in cases where our own conduct has obviously been a factor contributing to the discord, but also when we appear to be perfectly innocent, at least on the surface. I remember a young lady who soundly berated me for some professional advice that in all innocence I had given to her mother-in-law. On probing within for my own fault, I found that only too often had I been guilty of hers. It was humiliating to discover this, but at once superiority dropped away and compassion arose instead. Whenever we do not like what someone else does, we are really disliking our own fault which we see in the other. If someone scolded a teetotaller for being seen drunk, he would not be annoyed, he would merely look blank or be mildly amused.

Finally Tenko San's teaching of Sange is applicable even in the case of the most deeply wronged people, as for example the American negroes. To suffer without retaliation will not alone bring reconciliation. Only love can bring that, and love is not possible without willingness to bear the burden of the evildoing in the other. If the negroes truly seek reconciliation with the whites they must admit, as Gandhi did, that they have brought their troubles upon themselves, by their own shortcomings, that is to say by their cowardice and their willingness to become the despised people that the whites told them they were. This may seem a terribly cruel thing to say. But the law of Sange—bearing the blame—is inexorable. If one is overcome with dizziness when standing on the edge of a precipice, the law of gravity has no pity, whatever the excuse one must perish. As long as the whites must take all the blame, only the exceptional ones will be able to forgive the negroes for allowing themselves to be the scapegoats.

And that shows the difficulty in training oneself to work in accord with the law of Sange. There is only one person one can train, and that is oneself. We may not wait for the other fellow to come half way. And it is our own nation, our own people that we must start with. We cannot delay for the other and we cannot consider whether we shall perish in the process. (The best we can do perhaps is to console ourselves with the thought that blood of the martyrs was the seed of the Church!) As nations are composed of individuals, Tenko San's teaching requires us each to look only within and to refrain from trying to make others into reformed characters, even those of our own nation. In the pages that follow there is ample evidence that this attitude of penitence very often does lead to the reform of the other, and this has been my own experience also, at least in personal matters. But we may not depend upon it having this result.

This is the aspect of Sange which has meant most to me from a practical point of view. But for those of Tenko San's disciples I met, I think the most important aspect is the need to expiate those evils by humble service. Toilet cleaning is undertaken not to make a more hygienic Japan, but because they seek to lower their pride, and service is given, not because there is no one else to do it—as would be the case in India—but for the sake of working without payment. But once again let me remind the reader that he must read the text and not depend upon any partial explanation of mine.

The widespread sale of *Life of Sange* led, two years later, to the formation of an association of lay disciples, Koyukai, Friends of Light.

Tenko San's fame also began to spread abroad, and he was invited to foreign lands to give his message. The first country visited was Taiwan, then under Japanese occupation. He preferred doing Takuhatsu to giving lectures and always tried to combine this with the lecture programme scheduled for him.

It was on his return from Taiwan that the first little house was given to Ittoen's members, or more correctly, to Light! It was down town in Kyoto.

He was next invited to Manchuria, then to Korea, and finally in 1927 to America. But knowledge of his existence did not spread to England. The visit to Manchuria later led to the establishment of a branch of Friends of Light there, and a legally incorporated branch of Kosenrin. This visit had a further sequel when the government asked Tenko San if he could nominate someone to settle in Manchuria in order to reclaim derelict farmlands. He chose a married couple who lived there and later in China for a total period of ten years. They built dams and made roads, and restored previously fertile land to productivity. Similar requests led to quite a number of other members going to the same country.

In 1927 twenty-five acres of land under the hills above Yamashina were given to Light, the little cottage from Kyoto shifted there, and a year later Kosenrin was made a legally incorporated entity—Kosenrin Foundation.

Tenko San had further trips abroad on invitation, one to Hawaii and one to Indonesia. But Manchuria and Taiwan appear to have been the foreign countries on which he left his greatest impression, probably because both were in Japanese occupation and many there used the Japanese language.

Meantime, the original community was increasing, not merely by the addition of new adults, but by the birth of babies, and the babies were growing into children. In 1933 a primary school was established in Kosenrin. This was followed by a junior high school in 1947.

In this year, Tenko San accepted an invitation to stand for, and was elected a member of, the Upper House of Parliament. Here he tried to persuade his fellow members that Japan must take on her shoulders the burden of the wrongdoing of other nations. Needless to say they did not listen to him and he spent most of his six years' term in silence.

The children were growing up. A senior high school was opened in 1952 and later on a university college course was started, to which professors from universities in Kyoto give their services without remuneration, the ex-Baptist minister lectures on Christian life and teaching and an ex-Shinshu priest on Buddhist life and teaching, both the latter being members of Ittoen.

In 1955 Tenko San's wife died, and in 1961 he himself suffered a slight cerebral haemorrhage from which he had practically recovered when I saw him in 1963. He was again ill in 1964 and also had a fall, but again he miraculously recovered and was well enough to take a five-hour car trip. By 1965 he could not talk a very great deal but he was always smiling and inexpressibly happy.

Transcribing the chapters that follow from dictionary-English into idiomatic-English has proved the most worthwhile and inspiring writing I have ever undertaken. It was not an easy task, but often I wished it would never end, for Tenko San's new road to old truths was not merely wonderfully helpful but it reoriented life. To write what he has told about his new life has been like living in the presence of a great modern day Exemplar, comparable to Mahatma Gandhi, one whose teaching cannot be doubted because he has proved the value in actual experience.

I have heard it complained that members of Ittoen are proud of their humility, proud of cleaning toilets and living without money. These complaints may be partly true, for the demon of pride is an insidious spirit, as Tenko San himself points out, and steals in under the guise of our noblest virtues. But even though these criticisms may have some slight justification, this does not invalidate Tenko San's teaching: the need for rebirth into a life without desire through the dying to self (the truth at the heart of all religious teachings), the need to take on our shoulders the responsibility for all evil in the world and the need to expiate it by humble selfless service. Very few of us can find it practicable to live without money, and Tenko San does not say this is necessary, but it is essential to hold our money as a trust for all. In our affluent societies it also may not be practicable to do menial work in other people's houses, but it is essential that all our work whether for payment or otherwise, should be done as a service and not for money or thanks.

Tenko San has the gift of telling anecdotes, and all those he tells are the result of actual problems about which people in distress have sought his advice. Through these stories recorded in the following pages we see how practical is the way of life that depends upon the Light alone, and how disarming the attitude of penitence. Further, reading of those who have really trusted the Light shames us into giving up our own petty worries and instead trusting ourselves and our affairs to the wisdom that holds the universe.

Now that this translation, or more correctly paraphrase, has been permitted, I earnestly hope that some day an English-speaking person who is also a Japanese scholar will translate all of Tenko San's writings. But to do this successfully, he will need to be not merely a Japanese scholar, but also one who has at least tried to put his teaching into practice in daily life, and find this new life. Such a one will not be easy to locate, for, as I was so often told, Westerners are too intellectual. They think only with their minds, not with their abdomens, and therefore do not understand inwardly.

When I said farewell to Tenko San before leaving Japan on the first visit, he handed me a copy of one of his books. I could not read it of course and I had not a cubic inch of space left in my luggage. I therefore gave it to a young man I hoped would profit from it. I have often wondered whether Tenko San hoped I would learn Japanese and profit from it myself, or whether despite my being a Westerner, he had a premonition I might help translate his message for the West. It is now offered to Light as Takuhatsu. May Light accept it, like toilet cleaning, in the spirit of the Gyogan Prayer.

Acknowledgements:
Acknowledgements are made to the following: to Ayako Isayama San, a member of Ittoen and the teacher of English in Ittoen's school, who painstakingly went through the manuscript with the original text to make sure that in transcribing the translation into idiomatic English, I had not made any deviation from the meaning of the original: to Miss Florence James, a publisher's editor who read my first version and suggested improvements: to the Ittoen Community which permitted me to reside as a guest for two months for the purpose of completing the manuscript to the satisfaction of the Kosenrin Foundation: to Mrs Jean Moreton Maddocks who designed the dust cover: to Yuzo Matsumoto San who put the dust cover design into Japanese style and made it ready for publication: to *Gandhi Marg* in which portions of the Introduction have already appeared: to Mrs Irene Ray, a professional proof-reader, who kindly gave of her time to read the proofs.

M. B. Byles,
Cheltenham.
N.S.W. 2119

CONCERNING THE CHAPTERS

The following chapters except No. 10 are taken from Tenko-San's *Life of Sange,* a collection of his talks given to meetings around 1920. The titles used in the original have been changed and summaries and footnotes added so that the English-speaking reader can follow the contents more easily.

M. B. Byles
M. Ohashi

Chapter 1

THE BIRTH OF ITTOEN

It has been announced that this talk is to be 'On Social Service'. I feel a little embarrassed because this title makes it sound like a lecture by some learned man. Our way of life was not the result of learned studies or research, and as soon as it is given a title, people prejudge it. Indeed, as soon as anything is given a name it tends to acquire a one-sided interpretation. Now I want to give this talk without your having any title in mind.

When a baby is born it is given a name; this is necessary for the sake of convenience. But with the name comes egoism and self importance. A wise person has said, 'Although one may be able to stand aside from various attachments, one finds it very difficult indeed to stand aside from concern for one's good name.' There is a proverb which says that 'A tiger leaves its skin after its death, and a man leaves his name'. It may not be altogether wrong for a person to be concerned about his good name. But the world's peace would be better served if people reduced their attachment to fame. Work is given us to do because it is necessary for the preservation of the human race. It does not matter who does the work. Therefore the names of the doers are not important. I sometimes feel embarrassed when I am given a good name.

If trouble arises because of the use of proper names, far more trouble arises because of the use of common names, especially abstract terms such as heaven and earth, life and death. I think the Buddha Sakyamuni was also worried about the misunderstanding that arises from the use of words, for he once said, 'I have never spoken a single word during all my forty-nine years', and in order to initiate his favourite disciple Maha-Kasyappa into the mysteries of Buddhism, he merely smiled. Indeed to 'know' or to 'name' must inevitably cause trouble. But on the other hand it would be very inconvenient if we had no names. Someone gave the name 'Ittoen' and someone else called us by the name of Tenko-Ka-Ko-Do (shortened to Tenko) and now we are called 'The Group for Social Service'. But, as I said, Ittoen was born accidentally. This is how it came about.

When I was young, I was rather a favourite in my district and the then governor expected great things of me. At the age of twenty, instead of being enrolled for military service I wanted to engage in some useful enterprise. In those days exemption from conscription was allowed to those who went to Hokkaido for the purpose of bringing waste land under cultivation. I therefore rented 2,000 acres of land there and persuaded 100 families from my district to go and settle there while certain others provided the capital. The governor encouraged me, made me a presentation and gave me a book called *Ho-Toku-ki* to guide me on how to run the project. I was very happy, and it may be said that the new life brought into being by Ittoen was conceived then, so that it really had its origin in this book. I settled down with the peasant farmers in Hokkaido, living in tents and working hard, day in and day out. This went on for three years. Then a clash of interests occurred between the peasants and the capitalists. The peasants were like my brothers with whom I was sharing my fortunes. The capitalists were like my patrons. But I was both capitalist and peasant worker simultaneously. It is a very different relationship than that existing today between capitalists and labourers, but careful examination shows certain common elements.

If I should take the part of the peasants a proper return on capital would not be forthcoming. If I took the part of the capitalists the peasants would not be able to make both ends meet. I did not want to be partial to either, and I was at a loss as to what to do. The guide book *Ho-Toku-Ki* taught four principles: industry, frugality, fitting into one's position, and giving way. The first three I thought I could act upon to some extent. But I could not see how the principle of giving way could be acted upon, for the interests of the capitalists and peasants were absolutely irreconcilable. If I wanted to concede to both sides, I would have to give away all I owned; then I would lose my property and my family would starve. If I wanted to protect my own interests I would not be able to take the part of either side. I could not see any way in which all three could get along together. Today a capital and labour co-operation committee has been established; but even despite this I hear that difficulty is experienced in reconciling both sides. It is easy to understand how a young man of twenty-one, despite all his studies and thought, could find no way out of the impasse.

A well-known business man recently said to me, 'Co-operation is a very difficult matter and can materialize only from an attitude of service like yours'. In order to break through the deadlock of my maiden enterprise, there was no alternative to my making all the concessions myself. I have always made a habit of carrying through even the smallest things right to the end. If I had compromised at that time by some makeshift measures, I might have made some money as a landowner; I might even have become the local member of parliament. But the habit of carrying things through right to the very end stood in my way.

I was absolutely determined to find the answers to the questions as to what is capital, what is interest, and what is this virtue of concession? The only way to get the answers was to give up all that belonged to me, and find the basic principle of the solution. It was my burning heart's desire to delve into these questions, and at the cost of my own life, find the method by which both sides might get along with each other

47

and the enterprise run smoothly. It was a terrific problem and a bitter trial, more especially as I had not attended even middle school and had no book to which to refer.

One day I buried a silver coin, watched it for half a day and observed that it did not increase in quantity. From this I came to the conclusion that interest is not rational. In a book written by Tsuneta Yano it is stated that if interest at 5 per cent per annum is paid on half a dollar for 2,000 years, the result would amount to tens of thousands of times more than the whole of the wealth in the world today. I therefore decided that the notion of payment of interest must have been due to a mistake.

In those days, the year 1900, socialism had come to the fore and I heard of Marx's *Das Kapital*. I also heard that the noted economist Hidematsu Tsuda had written a book *The Principle of National Economy*, that he had put the question, 'What is Price?' and had found that the answer was, 'Price is determined by the relation between demand and supply'; this he found arose from the mental state of the people, but the mental state must be studied alongside philosophy, and philosophy depended upon religion. At that point, it was stated, he came to his wits' end and threw down his pen. A definition of price simply could not be found. Later I happened upon the book in a library. I found the bit about price; it seemed to be somewhat equivocal. I remember the author's ending, 'I do not think that this book is complete, but a better conclusion will be derived from further study'.

This seemed reasonable. But my nature would not let me set the problem aside thus only half solved. My task was not to study the state of affairs as they now were, but as they could be. Whatever scholars might have said about the matter, or however history might explain it, was not my concern. I wanted to attain an immovable faith which could neither be shaken by any situation nor blindly bow before public opinion, a faith that would stand up to all situations and would be able to judge the justice or injustice of public opinion or create a new public opinion. If I had not been certain that I should find such a faith, I would not have undertaken such a nonsensical study, but would have lived in the same way as my friends. The solution of this problem was a matter of life and death to me. I blindly went on with my studies. If my study of Ho-Toku-Ki could be called the time of conception of Ittoen, then my bitter agony at this time might be called the birth pangs.

Until the time when my new life was born, various things had been taking place both inwardly and outwardly. The end of my old life brought the tragic knowledge that two men who are to one another as intimate as brothers, may nonetheless be striving against each other in actual life.

I shut myself up in a room in a Kyoto hotel without eating for about two days. A serious-minded friend, Sugimoto, brought me Tolstoy's book *My Religion*. It was exactly the book I needed. I read it at one stretch. Towards the end of the book I saw the words, 'Die if you want to live'. The word 'die' seemed to strike my very heart. It had not the utilitarian sense of the 'One can live if one is determined to die', or 'Risk all expecting to gain all'. The word 'die' as used here seemed to mean 'To live by overcoming others would be equivalent to the death of those overcome', that is, of the whole, and that if the whole were to live I should be satisfied even though I myself might die. All of us are merely like bubbles on the surface of the water of the whole. Even though the individual dies nothing of the whole vanishes. I was also struck by the thought, 'To die means to get rid of delusions'. When a man awakens he becomes the whole itself. I said to myself, 'Well, let me die'. I felt no strain, but rather as if I had leaped into the vast expanse of the whole world, the Unbroken Self, or as if I had been reduced to the Immortal Reality. It was a breathing in of all Being, or in religious terminology, a rebirth.

I was a business man, and this awakening had arisen because of the practical problems of life. But my studies also showed that I must place myself as regards my family in the position of Roto—homelessness and pennilessness. Therefore the first matter I had to deal with was the practical one of family relationship. I decided that it must be as if I had died. I resolved to abandon my home, apologize to my ancestors for losing my estate and ask pardon of my wife and children for being unable to support them, exactly as if I had in fact died. On that same day, I determined to be as one dead.[1] I threw myself on the mercy of God, left the hotel and went out onto the street to become a man of Roto.

Just at this time I had received a telegram from the head family of my native district to attend a conference of relatives to discuss ways and means of relieving the sad plight of this family by reason of failure in business. I took a ticket to Maibara, which was as far as the small money I had in hand would carry me, and the remaining miles I walked. As I sat on the rocks by the roadside, I must have cut a very lonesome figure, like a corpse in a coffin.[2] But so far from feeling like a corpse, I was pleasantly cheerful, for the future was like a plain broad highway before me. The problem of the relatives sank into the background and appeared only as a private nightmare of their own, caused by their own fears and perplexities.

I entered the conference room with a peaceful mind and a penniless purse.

After the usual greetings we came straight to the point by my asking the headman, 'What on earth troubles you?'

'I can neither pay off my debts nor collect the loans due to me,' he replied.

'And you are asking my opinion as to what to do?'

---

[1] Tenko San's family and his wife's family were people of position and wealth. By thus leaving them he was not leaving them homeless and without means of livelihood. Moreover under the joint family system of Japan, the family would automatically care for them. In this respect the position was the same in the days of Gautama the Buddha.   M.B.B.

[2] The seated position for the corpse is the custom only in some country places of Japan.   M.B.B.

'Yes, none of the others had any ideas and that is why we wired to you.'

'Well, recently I have found a very good way out of the difficulty. But I don't think I'll tell you because I am afraid it would be impossible for you to believe it.'

'Please tell me, for no one has suggested any alternative.'

'Then I will tell you. First, this is not a matter on which you ought to ask the help of any of your relatives.' I looked around at those present and they all seemed to agree with me. But as I went on, 'It is also a matter towards which the relatives should not remain indifferent,' their faces began to cloud while the headman's face which had formerly clouded, now brightened.

I looked at him and asked, 'Can you do as I tell you?'

'Please tell me.'

'My advice is—give up your holdings to your creditors to pay your debts even if this leaves you penniless, and as to the loans due to you, wait until the debtors bring the money of their own accord.'

'That would mean we could not make a living, could we?'

'If you cannot make a living, then follow me.'

'But you haven't much money, either, have you?'

'So far from having much, I am now penniless.'

'That is all the more reason why I cannot follow you, isn't it?' The headman's voice was getting angry.

My words must indeed have seemed to him to be insane, especially as I now continued, 'I'll support you as long as I live. If we must die, I'll die first. All will be well if we are on the right road, even though we do die.'

The headman now certainly regarded me as crazy and said laughingly, 'We'll have some food; you seem hungry.'

However, I did not take even a cup of tea. If I had taken so much as a mouthful, my actions would have belied my words. I considered that to provide this food he must have concealed his property from his creditors, or else have asserted his rights by force. If I ate or drank with them I felt I would be yielding to the devil, and this I was determined not to do. I told them this and then unceremoniously took my leave.

This story may seem rather like play-acting. But in view of the situation and anxiety over the future of the head-family, it was far from play-acting. I was desperately serious. World War I (1914-1918) robbed millions of people of their lives and devastated European cultivation built up over hundreds of years. Japan had an unprecedented boom. The newly-rich and overnight millionaires came to the fore. They boasted of their success as if it were the reward of their own ability and industry. Then two years ago there was a sudden reaction; the economic world was seized with panic, and many went bankrupt. The bankrupts tried to conceal their property and apologized for their failure. People came to believe that it was foolish to pay honestly.

According to this degenerate commercial morality my conduct at the time of the head-family's failure must indeed have seemed both foolish and insane.[1]

That evening I could find neither a place to stay the night nor a meal to fill my stomach. I felt I could not accept a meal offered by a friend, and for the night's lodging I went to the precincts of the shrine of the tutelary deity of the town. I sat on a thin cushion on a verandah in imitation of Zen meditation, and sometimes I walked around the place. This continued all night and the next day and the next and the next. That is to say I stayed there three days. I became thin and dazed by reason of not having eaten for so long. Sometimes I wanted to give in. I thought that all that remained was to die, and at this thought I felt dizzy and staggered. But then I recalled that what I had done was the result of many years' examination, that the fire within had not been extinguished and that the protection of Heaven was so strong that it would sustain me in my resolution to the very end. My tired body sat up through the third night. The fourth day broke and with it a baby's cry came to my ears.

[1] This episode took place in 1903. M.B.B.

A sudden thought arose, 'How if I cried like a baby? The baby is crying and its mother's breast must be full of milk. Perhaps she is too busy to come to the baby. If the baby did not cry and in consequence starved to death, how great would be the mother's grief. Crying must be essential. To suck the mother's breast is not to struggle for existence, or to overcome others or to battle against them. It makes both mother and baby happy. There is no milk before the baby is born. It is only by its birth that milk arises. The baby does not strive to gain the milk, nor does the mother strive to provide it. Both are nourished by the grace of nature. And food for mankind must be provided in exactly the same way. But by reason of his unnatural actions mankind has lost the grace to which he is entitled. Someone may even now be making ready to give me some food. Of course I do not want to live by force, but only by the permission of Heaven. Then in what way should I cry like the baby? Is it good for me to stay here?

Just then I saw a sunflower, the flower that turns its head towards the sun in its journey across the sky. I thought 'I should move my body only to the place where my food is ready. To show my state of hunger does not mean a struggle for existence.' Having reached this conclusion I stood up and walked into the town. It was early in the morning and the houses were mostly closed. About one-and-a-half blocks away a small quantity of rice had been dropped in a line across the road, presumably from a rice bag. I thought there could be no objection if I picked it up. This I did, grain by grain and washed it in a brook nearby. Then I borrowed a small stove from a relative, and boiled the rice which made something less than three cups of weak gruel. Having eaten it I returned to the shrine where I stayed one more night.

Next morning I passed by the house of a family with whom I was intimate. A clerk was sweeping the garden and he greeted me. I returned the greeting and went into the garden. The mistress of the house came out and said, 'You haven't had breakfast yet, have you? Do please come in.'

I continued to stand outside in the garden and she again eagerly asked me to come in. I said, 'Please listen to me. I cannot eat if it will cause your available food to decrease, nor if you have to make up for what I have eaten. I can only eat if it causes no trouble to anybody, and if my eating makes you live at ease.' What I meant amounted to saying, 'Please have faith in God, please be frugal, please be kind to others. And then I can eat.'

Two years before the mistress had lost both her husband and daughter. The family then had extensive trade connections and many employees. But owing to heavy debts the business had got into a rather bad way, and she had often consulted me about its affairs.

I heard afterwards that news of my unusual behaviour had spread through the small town and that this mistress had been very anxious about me. She now said, 'I'll do anything you say so long as you have a meal.' I then agreed to come in and eat.

The meal was ready, spread in the dining room, but I sat in the kitchen beside the maid and asked her for the remains of the boiled rice at the bottom of the iron pot she was cleaning and ate it. I had a full stomach for the first time in five days. Moreover, I was free from debts and obligations. With stomach full, I felt as if I could move about like a baby. I began helping. I cleaned the small table, wiped the cups, put things in the cupboard, and swept the garden. I then went in the backyard where there was a warehouse in which articles were scattered about and a dirty privy. My work for the day was to sweep and clean them. The mistress and men and maid servants watched my behaviour in silence. I stayed at the house that night and continued with the same work for three days. The third day was the end of the month, and according to the custom of the country they offered me a bowl of buckwheat. At the bottom hidden under the buckwheat were two eggs. I was deeply touched that they were so eager to make me live.

That night the mistress called me and expressed her sincere thanks. 'I have heard many preachers over this last twenty years. But I have never experienced such a feeling of gratitude. Apart from myself all the employees have changed. They have become diligent and serious. At the rate this goes on the precarious position of my family affairs will surely improve basically. I think the deceased members of my family must have inspired you to protect our house. I thank you very much indeed.'

I was most astonished at what she said, and quite overwhelmed. When I ate the remains of that rice at the bottom of the iron pot, it seemed to me that I had overcome the world, but also it meant the solution of my own problem. Now it turned out to be a double victory, for my spontaneous action had both encouraged other people and retrieved a house from decline.

Thus after several years of study of the problem, and after renouncing both my own self and my family, I had been the instrument for raising all. As well my own soul and body, tiny existence as it was, had been given new food and clothing, and as a result of natural and spontaneous action had exerted an influence on outer surroundings. It was all totally unexpected.

When Christ said he had overcome the world, what he said was literally true. The essential Essence of myself was immortal and it was from the Immortal that my tiny body had come into being in this world. It was through this new life from realization of the Immortal that my love for my wife and children could be fulfilled. Further, if a house could be retrieved from decline through this new life lived within the Immortal, surely a whole country could also be restored from ruin by the same means. The words of Christ 'In three days I will raise up the Temple again', were not vain boasting at all. When the Buddha Sakyamuni laid aside his crown never to take it up again, and instead took his begging bowl and did

Takuhatsu,[1] he was merely acting in accord with natural law.

When we have taken up the lowliest position in life, we have really attained the highest, for in this lowliest of positions all our prayers are fulfilled. In this lowliest state one can live independently of others, but at the same time relieve others from their sufferings. How gracious is this Law of Being. It is incomprehensible that people should assert that money is necessary for mission work. All man's knowledge can never produce such a mysterious power. Light embraces all good and excellent things within itself. It had already made me completely safe. It had shown me a new way in which I should travel along the road of life. I realized now that I should go here, there and everywhere to do Takuhatsu, 'begging', or more exactly rendering humble service, here, there and everywhere, because man's distress exists everywhere.

Now for many years I have done Takuhatsu, odd jobs and domestic chores in various houses. I once asked a Buddhist priest, 'What was the Takuhatsu of Buddha Sakyamuni?' He explained briefly and added, 'I heard that on one occasion a disciple of Sakyamuni asked him whether monks ought to go begging in lean years and that Sakyamuni had replied that then, most of all, monks should go begging. All the same, my own opinion is that in lean years we ought *not* to go begging.' When the priest said that I knew he would never understand the meaning of Takuhatsu according to Buddha Sakyamuni. Even I have discovered that it is most of all for declining houses that I must do Takuhatsu, and go alms-gathering.

Since then I have to some extent read both the Bible and the Buddhist Scriptures. These show that those who are accounted saviours and saints prove the rightness of this life

[1] In Japanese Buddhism begging and Takuhatsu have the same meaning. The monk takes his bowl in both hands and receives rice or money from various homes and in return prays that people may be disillusioned. As already explained Takuhatsu in the Ittoen sense takes a different form in that it means humble selfless service, but the underlying idea is the same.   M.O.

of Takuhatsu. I was then thirty-two years old and this was the time that the babe conceived when I read *Ho-Toku-Ki*, was now born. When this new life was born and made manifest to all, my family, my relatives, my friends and my neighbours all called me a lunatic and were much embarrassed. This state of affairs continued for two or three years. Now seventeen years have passed. Times have changed. People have now reached a dead end, as it were, because of depending entirely upon money, power, and knowledge, and hence it is that I am asked to give a lecture like this.

As to the title that this lecture was given 'On Social Service', you can judge my thoughts about it by the story of the birth of the Ittoen way of life. I did not come upon this way of life by studying difficult books, nor by deep thinking. What I then began came naturally, and I am satisfied that I must continue with the humble work I did on the first day of this new life. Though requested to explain the meaning of this new way of life, I feel there is some danger of degrading it by making speeches instead of doing humble work in silence.

Although the need for non-possession is for me absolute, I cannot shirk my responsibility when I am entrusted with anything, and I do not say it is wrong to have possessions. I only say it is not necessary to own anything at all. Because it is not wrong to possess things, I must show in practice how one must handle what one is entrusted with. I have not retired from the life of the world, but I have ceased to depend upon it. I may not enforce my way of life upon others, but also I may not be a coward when called upon to perform some worldly duty. I should be like a wooden gong that sounds only when it is struck and otherwise is silent.

As I came from the world of business and problems concerned with actual life I am very sensitive to the problems facing the social order of today. I think I have found a practical method for solving these problems. That is why, when I am requested to do so, I tell people about this method. The way may seem precarious and the method have many weak

57

points, but I am satisfied that both are perfectly clear. They mean going back to being the lunatic that people then thought me. I have made many good friends anxious because of my new life, but the time will come when they, too, will feel completely happy about it.

Chapter 2

A TALK AT THE FIRST
HOME OF ITTOEN

I am glad to have a chance to talk to you again after such a long time, and I expect there are new members here today as well as visitors who want to hear about Ittoen.

Now Ittoen is not derived from any philosophy or religion. It is an experiment which came into being spontaneously and independently, and I proceed only as directed by Light. Like Ittoen, this house came into being quite unexpectedly some six years ago and there is no telling what the future may hold. Visitors sometimes ask us what our religion is and what our method and objective. I am always at a loss as to how to answer for I have no definite philosophy. Ittoen's way of life can never be understood with the intellect, and members should never try to explain it intellectually. It can be understood only by living it.

It is like the story I once heard of an old man near Nagoya who genuinely liked repairing roads. He used to go to roads which were under repair and find someone to work as his partner in carrying straw baskets of gravel. He always worked without pay and he became very well known in the district. Once an official asked him what pleasure he found in doing this work. By way of reply the old man put the stick of the straw basket over the official's shoulder saying, 'Try it for yourself and you will understand'. Ittoen's way of life is like that. You can understand it only by practising it for yourself.

But in order to practise it *successfully*, there must be something more—a firm determination and a very real doubt concerning the old life. If a man has no doubt concerning his old life it is useless for him to attempt Ittoen's, for complete humility is utterly essential for this way of life.

In a sense this house has no ruler. But at the same time its door will be opened only for the one who is humble. If a person says nonchalantly, 'I may as well go and see Ittoen', neither he nor ourselves will be happy. But this is not to say that the Toban[1] in charge of welcoming guests will not treat the visitor courteously no matter what the motive with which he comes. A Toban will always thank a guest for coming, for he must assume that he will at least have some sympathy for Ittoen's way of life or he would not have bothered to come. Even if a visitor came merely to abuse us we should still treat him kindly, for in so doing we demonstrate one aspect of our way of life.

However, even though goodwill should always be extended to a guest you should never go into long explanations as to what Ittoen is, and especially never to one who does not come with a serious intention. If the explanation given is not very clear the questioner will only become more confused and may very well trip you up in your words. Goodwill should also be accompanied by a firm but gentle attitude so that the visitor leaves with a feeling of the inadequacy of his own way of life. But a Toban will not attain this attitude by human wisdom or by taking thought. It will come of itself but only by humility and prayer.

And now let me tell you of Fugen, one of Ittoen's members who went out to pursue a life of Roto or homelessness and intended to start by helping on the roads.

All one morning he worked on a certain steep road helping to push people's carts uphill. A paid labourer was doing the same work and he accused Fugen of poaching on his territory.

[1] A Toban is a director in charge of some aspect of the practical life of Ittoen. Tanko San was a general Toban.   M.O. and M.B.B.

When Fugen said he was doing the work without pay the labourer became angrier still, saying, 'Working without pay makes you all the more to blame'. Fugen realized that his objection was perhaps justified, so he left that road and went into Yamashina. Here, despite his willingness to work without pay, he could find no one who wanted to give him any work to do. This often happens to the beginner in Ittoen's life. He recollected that I had said, 'No family will let you do Takuhatsu for them if you have any thought that you are doing them a favour. You will be given work only when you ask for it very humbly, as a favour to yourself and not to them.'

In many cases the man who does Takuhatsu expects to be given food and lodging. This is as bad as expecting payment. Naturally, people are reluctant to give work to someone who is unknown to them. In such a case the novice may very well become depressed. The sun does not take compassion on him, nor does it delay its setting until he has obtained work. Darkness and hunger close in upon him. He has neither rice-ball nor lodging. He has only loneliness. Life has at last become very serious. He should not try to escape but swallow the experience to the very dregs. What should he do? Neither trying to think things out, nor any philosophy will help him one iota. He is utterly shamed, utterly helpless. All his conceit is dead. There is only one road open. He turns to prayer. This at last is true self-discipline or Shugyo.

Shugyo is learning to live like a Bodhisattva (one who renounces the bliss of Nirvana to return to earth again and again to help all sentient beings). I once said that when you come up against a blank wall in your practice of the homeless life of Roto, you should adopt the attitude of a beggar. By a beggar I mean one who is completely down and out without even a pretence of cleverness. Then you complete your humiliation by asking some family if they will give you the remains of their rice and a resting place for the night under the eaves[1]

---

[1] Japanese houses have eaves wide enough to protect lath and plaster walls, the laundry—and beggars—from the rain.   M.B.B.

of their house. True independence does not call for a proud attitude. When a man sincerely desires to serve all people, and can find neither food nor resting place, and yet feels that his body may still be of use to Light, he should not treat it foolishly, for it has been entrusted to him by Light. If the family of whom you beg for the remains of the rice refuses to give it, that does not matter. You should at least ask once as a favour. True independence means willingness to ask for your bare necessities.

To return to Fugen, after being unable to get work in Yamashina he went to a small village and stood in front of a farmhouse like a beggar. An old lady came out and he asked if he might sleep in a corner of the outhouse. She seemed impressed and gave him food, but he still asked to sleep only in a corner of the outhouse. In the morning he saluted the family and thanked them for their kindness. They were surprised and thought he must be the son of a rich man. He then worked in the house for about a fortnight, and they all became quite familiar with the meaning of Ittoen life.

Although the work done under the name of Takuhatsu may be the same outwardly as ordinary work, the spirit in which it is done is quite different from that of work for which there is payment. A man who truly wishes to do real Takuhatsu must first of all die to self, abandon all things and regard his body not as his own but merely as entrusted to him for the use of others. When he regards his body as a trust it is not his own desire which makes him seek for someone to protect it.

Then it is that a radiance seems to shine through his personality. His face and way of thinking are changed so that when asking for work his attitude is different from the attitude of those who ask from a self-centred motive. Humility and goodness show in his behaviour. Even though he may not get food and lodging he gets control of himself. Fasting for a day or so and sleeping in the open air only serve to train him. And being under the direction of Light, his presence influences others.

Fugen was like that. A member of that farmhouse family once said to me, 'Fugen San always settles our family troubles. A quarrel between father and son, or among brothers, ceases as soon as the sound of Fugen San's footsteps is heard at the entrance.'

While Fugen was working on that family's tea-plantation, Oda, another member of Ittoen, was also working there, when a visitor arrived and started to ask him about the philosophy of Ittoen. Oda replied, 'Work before talk and be a willing serf'. He then suddenly realized that he himself had spent the morning reading and that he was now talking instead of working. He was an honest man. He saw at once that he was not practising what he preached. He jumped up saying, 'Excuse my rudeness. I am neglecting my work on the tea-plantation', and he rushed off. The visitor was taken aback, but after a second's hesitation followed after him and started picking tea with him so that he might hear more about Ittoen. Oda's action was like that of the old man who favoured repairing roads. A Toban in charge of guests at Ittoen should act similarly. The visitor who is really in quest of truth is the one who says to the Toban, 'Please let me do some Takuhatsu with you'. A member of Ittoen should always have both firmness and a tender heart. Light is then certain to protect and help him.

Honen, the founder of the Jodo sect of Buddhism, once sent his disciple, Shinran, to take part in a debate on religious principles convened by certain other sects. Shinran did not enter into the debate but merely sat at the back and wept. Some of Honen's disciples asked their Master why he did not send an eloquent preacher instead of such a man as Shinran. He replied, 'Only Shinran could have done what he did. It was very good that he merely wept and returned without arguing.'

This story shows the mature character of Honen and his deep insight into the purity of the faith of Shinran who refused to be drawn into futile philosophical disputes. A

Toban at Ittoen should have the same faith and reticence as Shinran.

One who wants to become a member of Ittoen should never think of his own self interest, but strive to find a way of devoting his life to the One Great Whole. In a sense Ittoen does not exist within this house. This house is only a gateway to the true Ittoen. You find Ittoen everywhere as soon as you give up your former self-seeking way of living, become baptized in the Light of Funi, the Light of Oneness, and are thereby resurrected. Thereafter your relations with your surroundings are reconstructed entirely, and you will find that your family, and your debts[1] (if any) are taken care of.

All that is necessary is to reorientate yourself by forsaking your lifelong self-centredness. Do not theorize or question. Instead, alter your attitude towards your family away from possessiveness. You will feel like a man when his temperature drops to normal after having had a high fever, or as if you had been suffering from giddiness and now become once more able to see things clearly. Your former common sense could never have brought you that feeling of coolness and clear vision.

And now let me say something about the role of Tobans or directors at Ittoen. Among other things, a Toban may be asked to take into his care someone's son or brother who has fallen into evil ways. The director will never put any blame onto the evil-doer, but will remember that it is he himself who is responsible for all the sins of the world. He should deliberately and consciously repent and so should all the other members of Ittoen and take on their shoulders the blame, expressing sorrow for their mistakes and seeking to expiate them by their acts. They must keep this firmly in their minds both when visitors come to Ittoen and when they visit people in their homes. When the so-called bad son or brother comes to Ittoen he naturally expects to be scolded and strictly supervised. When he meets the Toban and finds that he takes upon himself all the blame for evil-doing, the so-called bad son or

---

[1] See the story of Mr S. told in the Introduction. M.B.B.

2 Tenko San in old age

brother will almost certainly become a new man almost over-night. This is principally due to Ittoen's members themselves bearing the burden of all evil-doing.

I have questioned several such young men who had been at Ittoen for some time, 'When you came here your parents said you had been behaving badly. But now you seem to be a good man. Can you tell me at what time you changed thus?'

The typical answer was something like this, 'The thing I least expected was that no one at Ittoen blamed me for the faults with which my family had always reproached me. Even when they did not openly blame me, I always felt their inward reproach and the home atmosphere gave me a ceaseless sense of oppression. I did not always want to sleep late in the morning, but I used to stay in bed because I dreaded seeing their unpleasant faces. I really did have a conscience and sometimes I would get up early and try to do some work, but they would sneer at me and make fun of me, so that I returned to my bad habits. When I was sent to Ittoen I had a feeling of strong resentment and was certain I could never endure staying in such a lonely place even for a few days. The strange thing was that after the first night my rebellious spirit died down under the gentle attitude of the Toban. What won my heart most of all was your remark, "I, too, am guilty of wrong-doing". To my ears, which had constantly had to listen to my own wrong-doing, your remark was enormously impressive. Furthermore, you never blamed me at all. Instead you blamed yourself. My rebellious feeling vanished. I slept peacefully the first night and woke to the sound of wooden clappers. I got up and worked at the sweeping and dusting like the others. Although my ankles ached a little during the sutra chanting at the morning service, I felt like a new man. The breakfast consisted merely of a mixture of rice barley and boiled vegetables. But it tasted very good indeed.

'Then the time for Takuhatsu[1] arrived, and all the people

[1] In those days nearly all the members went out every day to houses in Kyoto and its outskirts to do Takuhatsu.   M.O.

got ready to go out. The Toban said to me, "Take a rest for a couple of days". But I felt as if I also wanted to do Takuhatsu and asked him to let me go with them. Since then I have worked every day, a most unexpected thing for me. I wonder why the situation appeared so different when I saw it from outside. I think I understand what you meant when you said there was another world. I feel very sorry for my family and want to let them know about this new life. You ask me at what moment I underwent a change of heart? Well, I think it would be at the time when you said, "I, too, am guilty of wrong-doing". At that moment I felt as if I had awakened.'

One evening I saw one such of these young men drawing up the steep road to Ittoen a cart laden with a gift of a large sack of rice. Since the dusting and sweeping and the morning service, this man had done a long day's work. He must have been tired. I was impressed by his diligence and said, 'How do you feel mentally and physically after working so hard?' He answered pleasantly, 'I am very happy'. I said, 'Tell me what impression you get when you go to houses to do Takuhatsu?' He answered, 'It depends upon the house, of course. But it makes me happy to find I am welcomed by every family. Knowing nothing of my previous idleness, they ask me to educate their children and express a hope that their employees will be influenced by my diligence. This makes me very careful how I behave, so that I am really being trained by them instead of by myself. They trust me implicitly—I suppose because I work without pay.'

When I hear young men of former bad reputation talking like this, I am filled with deep gratitude. It is very wonderful that youths can get rid of longstanding bad habits and in consequence see another world altogether, and know that this has happened without any preaching from me, but solely because of the all-pervading Light. The reason Light can have this effect is partly because Ittoen members practise Takuhatsu with a feeling of sorrow and repentance, but also because neither Toban nor members blame others, but always themselves shoulder the responsibility for all human evils.

Rhetoric is not necessary for Ittoen, and we should never act as if we were clever persons. Rather, we should regard ourselves as fools, always seeking to learn from others. Ittoen may be described as a school where one learns to act as a poor man and a fool. Had I been a clever man I might have lived a very different kind of life. But being quite uneducated, all I could do was to enquire into my own faults. As a result of this enquiry all I could then do was to throw myself before Light.

Before this building of Ittoen came into existence my only dwelling place was in the street, as it were. My abode was always transitory. It changed from one house to another. When a friend, let us call him A, came to the house where I was working and wanted to do as I was doing, I passed over to him my work at that house and went on to another; when a second friend, B, wanted to follow my way of living, I again passed over my work and went on to a third house, where I would in turn give my work to C and so on. I also went round to people's houses and talked to them about faith in Light. In those days the practice of Takuhatsu was far more basic than it is now that we have been given this building and there are both advantages and disadvantages in the change. When there are many serious-minded men living here, they are a great help to the young men I have told of who have fallen into evil ways. But when the serious-minded are few, these young men will be hindered instead of being helped.

One cannot be trained to be like a Bodhisattva (who re-nounces bliss to help all beings) in such a building as this if one regards it as a shelter. The base for a member of Ittoen must always be the street. He goes to various households when requested, works for them all day long, and they offer him meals, baths, clothes and lodging. He should come to this house only to introduce other people, or to consult with a Toban, or to attend meetings. A Toban should remain here[1]

[1] Ittoen's way of life has altered a great deal outwardly since this was written.　　　　　　　　　　　　　　　　　　　　　　　　　M.B.B.

only when on duty. If he acts without taking these things into consideration, Ittoen will gradually become a kind of temple or church subject to all manner of rules which may not be infringed. I earnestly hope that all members will look upon every house they visit for Takuhatsu as Ittoen, and this building only as its gateway. If they do not do this Ittoen cannot be an entrance to the Light of Funi, which is Two but not Two, the very essence of Buddhism.[1] If one should take the gateway for the base, one can neither realize the true worth of this life nor testify to its mission.

Even though a member leaves his family, he should not on this account retire from the world. On the contrary, he now goes into all houses instead of one to prove this new way of living. The youths I have told you about were not the only ones changed as a result of coming to us. Their families also were changed, although perhaps unconsciously. This change takes place more easily when members, especially Tobans, follow the basic principles I have spoken of.

---

[1] A central teaching Mahayana Buddhism is the Great Oneness in which Nirvana and Samsara are found to be the same. Two but not Two expresses the same paradox. M.B.B.

Chapter 3

FUKUDEN OR SELFLESS TREASURE

You have asked me to give a talk about Fukuden.

Fukuden is a Buddhist term, but I have not studied the meaning given to it by Buddhist scholars. I use it because it makes me feel at ease. 'I prefer Fukuden to property', has become my motto. I prefer it because one can depend upon Fukuden; one cannot depend upon property.

When I was a child my father used to say, 'Even though a man has excellent qualities he may well become a beggar if he lacks one thing'. By 'one thing' he meant the ability to make money. He himself was very clever at money-making. Also he was a good man, kind and willing to serve others, and consequently revered by a great many. But throughout his life he never saw the fallacy of regarding the ability to make money as of foremost importance. It is not my father alone who was misguided in this regard. His district, his country, perhaps the whole world regard money as the most important thing. I am afraid that not in the measurable future will the proverbs, 'Money is Almighty', and 'A golden key opens most locks', become ridiculous.

World wars have their origin in money and power. Yet money continues to be regarded as essential. Saints of old have said, 'Do not worry about how to feed and clothe yourself' and 'Food and clothes come naturally to those that seek the Truth'. But people regard these sayings as outdated. Even in churches and temples there is no attempt to verify them. So it is no cause for wonder that my father regarded money-making as of foremost importance.

My new way of life shows that even if we did not have money we should nonetheless not become beggars, and it testifies to the sayings of the Saints. It also shows that the one thing necessary is not money, but Truth or Light. In this talk I do not intend to tell how this new life came into being beyond pointing out that it is not based upon trying to preserve one's life, except in so far as Light permits one to live and one's living profits others. This being so there is obviously no need for money or property. When a man embarks on this new life, serves others for the sake of Light alone, those served invite him to eat and give him the means of living. I may accept food and even clothes and lodging when what is given is offered to God with a devout heart. In return I pray that the giver may receive Fukuden a thousandfold.

It was on the occasion of such a gift that I began to use the term Fukuden. A man's spiritual and material wealth are changed to Fukuden when he realizes that a life of non-possession which outwardly appears precarious is in fact the most solid and stable. Fukuden is the joy and peace that a person finds within his heart when in consequence of this understanding he begins to give up acquisitiveness and greed. But if we regard material things also as Fukuden this is not altogether wrong, for when things that are necessary are given, these become Fukuden. On the other hand, if we expend material things wrongfully the door of Fukuden will never be opened for us. Therefore Fukuden is both a purified heart and purified material things.

Earthly property, if improperly spent or used up, can never again be restored no matter how reasonable our requirements. But Fukuden is limitless, and because it belongs to all it does not cause envy or jealousy. The meaning of Fukuden is exactly expressed by the words of the Bible, 'Lay not up for yourselves treasure upon earth where moth and rust doth corrupt'.

Earthly wealth can be measured. Fukuden cannot. That is why so few people rely on Fukuden. Those who understand its meaning sometimes get impatient with those who do not. Misunderstanding is inevitable.

I was once placed under police surveillance as a man having dangerous thoughts. I was somewhat of a burden to the Thought Department, but notwithstanding this, all the staff treated me kindly and trusted me. Many people, some themselves under police surveillance, would stay at Ittoen. Even the police sometimes asked me to take care of persons who had fallen into evil ways. Nonetheless they continued to wonder what I meant by Fukuden. For example how did we get food if Fukuden meant wealth in the heart? I wished I could make my ideas understood; for I did not want to be regarded as belonging to some Red group, nor did I want it supposed that I was receiving assistance from a white capitalist group. Certain people suggested I was living from the profits of a mine with which I had been entrusted, whereas in fact I was giving it some of my Fukuden.

Also it was natural that the police wanted to know how we could do Takuhatsu all the year round, and also allow any who came to Ittoen to stay and eat without charge.

The duty of the police to supervise those with dangerous thoughts required them to find out about our economic resources. Thus every time a new official arrived, Ittoen came up for discussion. I was once doing Takuhatsu at a certain house when I was called to the telephone. The following conversation took place.

'Is that Mr Tenko Nishida?'

'Yes, this is Tenko.'

'This is Sergeant X of the Police Thought Department. I want to talk to you about Ittoen.'

'Certainly, shall I come to your office?'

'By rights, I ought to visit *you*. Nonetheless I would be very glad if *you* came to *me*.'

'Good! I'll come at once.'

I went round immediately and the conversation continued.

Officer, 'Glad to see you.'

Tenko, 'I'm sorry I've taken so long to come.'

Officer, 'I hear you go to great trouble to help people. Will you please tell me the way in which you are doing this.'

Tenko, 'Your question is rather vague. Could you please ask me item by item.'

Officer, 'Then I'll ask you about something which seems to me very strange. Is it true that you say one can live without earning money?'

Tenko, 'Yes, I do say that. But I dare say that when, due to wrong thinking, a person is at sixes and sevens with himself, then money may be indispensable to him. Also, I do not think it is wrong to possess money so long as it is properly used. But I do say it is not indispensable. For my present way of life it is not necessary. I further assert that people should give up attachment to money.'

Officer, 'True, but nonetheless it does sound rather extraordinary to say that money is not indispensable, doesn't it?'

Tenko, 'I agree. But nonetheless money is not necessary for our way of life.'

Officer, 'Don't you require money to travel by train?'

Tenko, 'True, but others bring me to the places to which I travel, for since I started my new way of life, I have no business of my own.'

Officer, 'Oh! But apart from that, surely you *ought* to have some business of your own, and help others only in your spare time.'

Tenko, 'A short while ago you 'phoned and you were glad that I could come to your office, weren't you?'

Officer, 'Yes.'

Tenko, 'If I had had my own business it would have been necessary for *me* to ask *you* to come to me.'

Officer, 'Yes, I suppose so.'

Tenko, 'So it would be difficult for a person to serve others if he had a business of his own to attend to?'

The clock struck twelve. The officer ordered lunch to be brought for me also, saying, 'Please have lunch with me.'

'Thank you, but I think I ought to be going.'

'I have a few more questions to ask. As you took the trouble of coming here, I should be glad if you would talk to me over lunch.'

I smiled, 'A little while ago you had the feeling that it was not possible for meals to be offered to me every day.'

'Yes, I admit I did.'

'During the ten years that I have been serving others day after day, not only have I been offered food like this but also clothing and lodging.'

'I begin to understand. A concrete example makes things clear. Please have lunch.'

The lunch was very good and we had a pleasant conversation. He was a most agreeable man.

The officer's doubts were due to his being unable to understand the meaning of Fukuden. If we cannot grasp its meaning, life has no basis. If we can, then the way out of all the world's difficulties is found.

No religion can stand without Fukuden as its basis. That Buddha or God will provide food is a fundamental law of being. When taken into account and acted upon it provides a solution for all problems. I sometimes hear people say it is impossible to engage in missionary work without money, and that for the purpose of such work an endowed foundation is necessary. I would say that exactly the reverse is true, and that if one has money one can never engage in religious missionary work successfully. If work is done by means of money, the result must smack of money. If it is done by means of power or position, it must smack of power or position. No religion resulting from such things can be relied upon. A true religion enables a man with empty pockets to save people from suffering. Real suffering is beyond the reach of succour by money or power or position. Those who effectively preach the need to trust the problems of life and death to God, do not need money or position, no, nor intellectual knowledge. The only worth while gospel is the one that can show how, without any of these things, a man can overcome the miseries of life and death, break through all barriers and find true freedom. In the midst of people at their wits end because of their erroneous notion that money, power and knowledge are necessary, the one who has found true freedom can roll about like a tank on a battlefield, unrestricted in body and mind. To be able to do this is the best way of teaching a religion. When a person can do this, he has found true salvation.

At one time a certain K., a young man little over twenty, came to me. He said,

'The other day I read a newspaper article from which I gathered that you could save a man in distress. Therefore I am hoping that you will come to the rescue of a man I know.'

'What is the matter with him?'

'He's a pitiful old man of about fifty. I met him in the precincts of Toji Temple, and I took him to my home to find a job for him but he could not get a suitable one. I am ashamed to say I am not independent. I am studying at a pharmaceutical college and depend on my wife's income as midwife. I brought the man back to my home, but when his stay was prolonged my wife began to complain, and because of my dependent position I could not assert myself. I was at a loss what to do when I chanced on the newspaper article about you. That is why I have come.'

I replied, 'If he has been reduced almost to being a beggar it would not be wise to bring him to Ittoen immediately. Personally, I would not mind his coming, but there are many types of people at Ittoen, and were he to come I am afraid that some of the less experienced youths might backslide. Therefore I shall go to him myself and go with empty pockets and in the state of Roto.[1]

[1] Roto means literally the homeless and penniless state of one living on the streets. But in Ittoen's use of the word it also means the spiritual state of one who is not attached to knowledge, self-pride, worldly love, nor resentful of suffering or other unpleasant states. This detachment is true freedom and emancipation.　　　　　　　　　　　　　　　　M.O.

K. then said, 'Shall I go and get him?'

'No,' I said, 'wait a moment. Take him back to the place where you found him. I'll visit him there if it is at all possible.'

K. left me. Next day was the festival day at the Toji Temple, the twenty-first of the month. Each month on that day there are large crowds, and I made a habit of going there to do Takuhatsu by helping the Kawamichi-ya branch noodle shop. While I was waiting nearby an elderly man came along and I saw him sit down on a stone. I walked up to him and said,

'Are you the man K. told me about?'

'Yes, he told me to go to the place where he had found me, and a teacher far greater than he would save me from my troubles. Are you that teacher?'

'I am not a teacher. But I myself was saved from my troubles without having a penny in my purse. Are you determined to try and copy me and be saved from *your* troubles as I was saved from mine?'

'I don't know what you did. But if it is at all possible I shall do as you tell me.'

'Well, it is just as possible for you as for me. Listen!'

'Yes, sir.'

'Imagine that you are to be saved from your troubles immediately, and do something to show your gratitude.'

'But I am not yet saved. I'll show my gratitude when I am—that is to say when I get a job and some money. At the moment I have nothing.'

'You have a hunting cap in your hand, but I haven't one in mine. As well you seem to have some rice-balls in your pocket and I guess you also have a few pennies.'

'Oh, such a poor cap! K. gave me these rice-balls for my supper and he also gave me some small change for a lodging in a doss-house.'

'Now just think. I have none of these things you possess. Further, when I was first saved from my misery, I was wearing poorer clothes than yours, and I didn't even have wooden

75

clogs. Since then, and with nothing more, I have been cease-lessly doing service out of gratitude, and I shall continue doing service out of gratitude in the future until the day of my death. Compared with me you are a far richer man.'

He was now looking at me amazed. The more he looked the more obvious it was that my belongings were less than his. Eventually he sighed, saying, 'I am now fifty; I have never heard that kind of talk in all my life. Do you really mean that, though I am at the bottom of my poverty, I should nonethe-less give?'

'Yes, although you have never heard of this in all your fifty years, the fact is that in all those fifty years you have never been saved. And this is the *only* way in which you *can* save yourself. You have failed to do the good you could have done, and your lack of virtue has brought you to this state of poverty. But now you are to be saved from it. Indeed, already you have *been* saved from it. Therefore, in gratitude you should give all your belongings to someone poorer than your-self.'

The old man breathed heavily with downcast blinking eyes. He seemed unable to understand my words, as though he had fallen into unexpected bewilderment. Silently I invoked Light, saying to myself, 'The old man has good reason to feel as he does. Who in all the world would have spoken to him in such a way? I should like to give him a job and lodging straight away. But no good would result from that. He has fallen into this impasse through lack of virtue. Without being given true salvation of spirit, would not food, clothing and lodging be merely a sorry makeshift?.'[1] Aloud I said, 'It is reasonable that you cannot understand. I therefore pray that you may obey my unreasonable orders. If only you would say "Yes", Light would at once shine in your soul. I pray you will not feel anxious. Feelings of anxiety are delusions. Please say "Yes" obediently and awaken from the darkness of fifty years.

[1] The Buddha of the Canonical Texts repeatedly says that all gifts are good but that the gift of the Dhamma (the Light) is the greatest of all gifts.   M.B.B.

On my life I assure you that you will find salvation. You must die, die now, and receive the grace of Light, full and abundant. Oh, merciful Buddha!'

The old man's mouth was firmly closed; his eyes seemed dimmed with tears; his folded hands were between his thighs; he sat firm as a rock. I sat quietly, 'Can't you think of yourself as having just died. After all you must die some time. Give your belongings to the poor and give service so long as you can move. Let us be glad that we can do this even at the brink of death. I won't let you die alone, you know.'

The tears almost fell from his eyes. When he spoke, his voice seemed to come from the depths of his heart, 'I'll obey you. I'll die immediately.'

'Then do as I tell you.'

'Yes.'

'You see that there are a great many visitors here, and that the place is littered with rubbish. I'll bring a broom for you. But first you must give your lunch and small change to a beggar, the poorest you can see. After that, sweep the precincts to the best of your ability, and after the people have left and the temple gates are closed, go to the main hall of the temple dedicated to St Kobo-Daishi and give thanks to him for your having been able to give service. Then stay for the night under the gate of the temple.'

'What shall I do after that?'

'I don't know any more than you. But I hope the Buddha will give you the direction. If not, then continue to sweep the precincts as long as you live. Now I have to go to Mount Koya; some people have asked me there. But I shall come back in about three days. I am sorry that I shall be sleeping on mats[1] myself while leaving you to sleep out of doors, but I must accompany the person who invited me. Here is some of the travelling money my host gave me. It is my duty to give it to you.'

[1] Japanese people sleep on a thin mattress on tatami mats on the floor.
M.B.B.

I fetched a broom from the noodle shop, gave it to the old man and then said goodbye. I saw him go into the crowd with a look of resolution on his face. I asked the assistant at the noodle shop to give him two bowls of noodles if he had swept up hereabouts. He readily agreed. I left for Mount Koya that evening.

After five days I returned to Kyoto anxious to hear about the old man who had seldom been out of my mind. I 'phoned K. By good fortune the man was at his house.

'What happened to him?' I asked.

'He is very happy. He says he has never been so grateful in his life.'

I drew a deep breath of relief, and asked K. to bring the man to me at once. I was impatient to know what had made him so grateful. An hour later the old man came.

'Teacher, thank you very much indeed. I am so happy.' His face was quite different from what it had been five days before when I met him sitting on that stone.

Without thinking, I said, 'Thank heaven! What have you done since then?'

'Listen,' he said, 'I gave my lunch and my money to poor people as you told me to do. They were very happy and so was I. I felt rather strange, for never before had I been thanked by others for giving them something. My feeling of happiness was inexplicable, for I felt no uneasiness about losing either my rice-balls or my money. After that I recalled that I had to sweep around the place, and I became absorbed in that until it grew dark. "Good heavens!" I said to myself. An assistant at the noodle shop who seemed to have been looking at me now came up bowing and saying, "You are tired, aren't you?" Whereupon he handed me two bowls of noodles. It was a strange experience to be given food without asking. It was as if St Kobo had given it to me, and I held my hands prayerwise before receiving it. Then I gave thanks to St Kobo and calm and mindful I passed the night under the temple gates as you had bidden me.

'About ten o'clock a policeman came up saying, "What are you doing here?" Then another strange thing happened. He did not make me timid; before this I used to become timid merely on hearing the sound of footsteps at night. Now I answered calmly, "Sir, today I listened to a teacher who told me about faith and I gave thanks to St Kobo. And now I am keeping vigil here for the night." The policeman nodded understandingly and left me silently without saying anything further. I felt as if I had become a new man.

'Next morning as I set to work sweeping again, the manager of the rice shop at the corner in front of the temple gate said to me, "You were sweeping here yesterday, and you are doing it again today. You seem to be a stranger. Have you come to live in this temple?" I replied, "No, I haven't." Then I went on to tell him about the teacher and what he said and all that had happened. The manager seemed quite impressed and said, "Come in and have some breakfast". I ate gratefully, and now with a full stomach I desired to render service in the same way at other places. I remembered a waterfall in the compound of the shrine of Inari where people come to bathe. I went there. As I was sweeping to express my gratitude, one person after another asked me why I was doing it, and I told them about your teaching. I was readily given both food and lodging. A man from Osaka, who came every day to bathe, said to me, "I have come here many times and yet I have never felt grateful. I have been tremendously impressed by your attitude of working with gratitude. Let me give you lunch every time I come and let me guarantee your lodging." But I did not forget what you said, "Even when invited to enter a house, stand at the gate, and sleep in one blanket even though you may be given two".

'I have continued to work with a grateful mind, and have always been given food, money and kind treatment. I remembered that you said you would meet me again in three days. But I could not come then. Now I return to you the money you gave me for lodging in a doss-house. I am very grateful.

I feel like a new man. I never noticed before that everyone in the world is very good-natured. Five days ago they all seemed devils. Thank you very much, teacher. I am now filled with confidence about living.'

I was amazed at how he had obviously found salvation. Two bowls of noodles were all that I had arranged for him to have. All the rest had come from Light. Inwardly I folded my palms in reverence for the grace that had been given. Aloud I said, 'Already, my friend, you are confident about living your life, aren't you?'

'Certainly,' he replied, 'and now I must be going.'

'Then go to Ittoen. I am off to Tokyo tonight, but will be back in two weeks or so. Take this note with you when you go to Ittoen.'

'Thank you, sir.'

I wrote a note about him on my visiting card and gave it to him.

The first thing I asked when I returned to Ittoen was how he was getting on. I was told that Kosugi San, as he was called, was a good-natured man and that he was happily looking forward to my return.

Kosugi San continued to work well and honestly, and in response to requests he also went to various places to do Takuhatsu. Then he became ill and died in his birthplace. His last years had all been spent in making people happy and his life had been abundantly blessed.

This story proves exactly the opposite of the contention that money and power are necessary for missionary work. It was precisely because I had no money that I could persuade this old man to do what he did. And it was also because this man had no money that he could start a new life. When the soul is awakened possessions both material and intellectual are of no importance. Good things come from all sides to such a one.

Further, those who give are also purified. In the Buddhist

5 The Worship Hall of Ittoen

6   Dining room at Ittoen

Scriptures known as the Vimalakirti[1] Sutra, such food is called Joban, that is, sanctified food from the Fragrant Country of the Blessed. The words of Christ 'Take up your cross and follow me', also embody the deepest meaning of Joban. There may be some difference of degree but all come from Light.[2]

It is interesting to apply Fukuden on the one hand and material property on the other to the economics of production.

Some people think our new way of life is effeminate and negative in that it aims to do all sorts of odd jobs by way of service instead of engaging in some specific industry or specializing in a definite subject. For this reason, such people contend that it does not offer a practical way of running affairs in this world of fierce conflicts.

Their objections are understandable, and we have given serious consideration to them. But though at first they may seem reasonable, we cannot agree they are valid. Experience has shown us that our way of life is not only manly and positive, but that it also contains within it the power to give a fresh start to one whose life seems to have come to a standstill.

Production presumably means increasing the number of things in existence. Now those who find flaws in our way of life are not increasing the number of things in existence; they are merely struggling to get things for themselves. After struggling thus they shout loudly that they have made a profit. Even when they engage in a somewhat dubious business they can always justify it so long as it brings a profit. Instead of worrying about the worthwhileness of their own work, they worry about ours.

Apart from the economics of the matter, the struggle for profits makes the struggler's mind mean and poor—the opposite is the poor in spirit spoke of in the Bible. People talk about

---

[1] Vimalakirti was a layman of superlative wisdom and virtue far surpassing that of the greatest of the Buddha's monk disciples and any Bodhisattva.   M.B.B.

[2] Tenko San said that it can save man's soul and body, and indeed his very life.   M.O.

improving their standard of living when what they actually do is to strive to satisfy a hungry ghost.[1]

When one eats with composure one can assimilate nutriment from so-called coarse fare, the digestive organs work well and excretion takes place as it should. But if one eats with a troubled mind, one cannot eat with relish no matter how expensive the food, and the digestive organs are dull so that they cannot take from the food the nourishment required.

Similarly, if one's mind and body are not in harmony one cannot be at ease even in a gorgeous mansion. One becomes the slave of a hungry ghost because of always wanting to acquire, wanting to possess. Everyone sees the folly of putting more into a sack without first mending the holes at the bottom, but they are apt to be unaware of the folly of grasping for more when by so-doing they always feel more discontented.

A few years ago European civilization was ravaged by a world war.[2] Should we accept such setbacks to civilization? All admit that the cause of the war was the devil of egoism and greed. Is it wise to retain that devil in our hearts and let it have its way? In our new way of life we wake up to the folly of such negative resignation. We refuse to resign ourselves to our minds and bodies becoming the slaves of egoism and greed. We determine to overcome that devil. Even though it has built up vast organizations this does not prevent it from being wholly evil.

Our new way of life begins by mending the rents in the sack—by defeating the devil of greed. It also demands that we should not engage in dubious forms of production and should cease to strive for greater and greater consumption. We try to live with perfect equanimity, as did the Buddha, so that we

[1] Popular Buddhism believes that people are reborn in various forms. One of these are the pretas or hungry ghosts. These hungry ghosts are pictured as having huge bellies craving to be filled, and pin-sized mouths incapable of taking food. They are the ghosts of people who as human beings were always grasping for more and more. Ceremonies for the hungry ghosts are very common in Japan.   M.B.B.

[2] The First World War, 1914-1918.   M.B.B.

assimilate nutriment from small quantities of food instead of overeating, and despite overeating trying to reduce our weight. We acquire such insight into Truth that instead of being driven helplessly before the devil of greed and egoism, we learn how to overcome it.

Politics, education and religion, especially religion, all seek for world peace and therefore have the same objective as our new way of life. But these seldom take into account the formidable barrier of egoism that must be overcome before peace can be achieved. This barrier hides from a man his own evildoing and the evil-doing of his country, and lets him see only the evil of others. Occasionally perhaps a man may be sufficiently truthful with himself to admit his own errors. But he excuses himself by saying that, though he may be at fault, others are worse, and that it is useless to reform himself if others do not do so also. He tells himself that if he practises Sange[1] by taking all the blame on his own shoulders, he will be ruined and his family starve. 'Give in,' says the devil, 'life in Heaven can be lived only after death.' If, despite what the devil says, he is still determined, he foresees his wife weeping with anxiety, his parents blaming him for undutifulness, his friends mocking him and saying he has gone mad. He realizes he will become an outcast from his religious sect, that he will lose his job, his clothes, and even a place to live. Then the devil says sneeringly, 'Can you bear it?'

Suppose that this man, filled with high inspiration, reminding himself of the cross and thinking of the Buddhist Sutra concerning self-sacrifice, still persists, the devil then changes his tactics. He now becomes polite and deferential as to a very wise man, saying in a sweet voice, 'Only you and I have a deep understanding of things. Suppose with firm resolution you take up your cross, it would end only in the deliverance of your own soul. You cannot save others, for people in

---

[1] See Introduction. Sange literally means penitence or repentance and holding oneself responsible for all the evils of the world both one's own and others' from time immemorial. The term also includes physical and spiritual practices to expiate these evils.   M.O.

general cannot do what you aspire to do. You would not want to save your own soul unless all are saved. From ancient times a number of people have passed this barrier, and you must admit that the world is the same now as ever it was. Your attitude appears strong, but it is really weak, for it is not a true denial of selfish greed. Under the pretext of taking up your cross, you are merely hiding a subtle form of egoism. Think it over, rely upon your sincere wisdom and deep prayer, and you will find that the miseries of the world today cannot be cured by your adopting the attitude of Sange.'

Being thus tapped on the shoulder, so to speak, that man may well begin to think that what the devil says may be true. Ironically, the argument about the selfishness of saving his own soul seems all the more valid because his reasoning faculty is good, and his prayer deep. Thus it is that, despite knowledge, will-power and prayer, and also despite his sincere wish to find the way, he may nonetheless be overcome by these plausible arguments, and turn back.

There is a proverb that says one betrays one's weakness when offered what one likes best. Enticed by the honey of the need to save all mankind and not merely himself, this man is led into revealing the innate egoism which he shares with all mankind. The devil laughs up his sleeve.

People make a great to-do about the need for helping and saving all. But as soon as one undertakes some practical work for others and tries to carry it through to a successful conclusion, sooner or later dissensions always arise. And sometimes the dissension never ends unless one side gives way completely to the other. Therefore if anyone undertakes such a practical work he must admit that conflicts are inevitable unless he can show a basically different social order far beyond the ordinary. Hence the need for a basic and radical reorientation of one's own life is essential before one can help others in a practical manner. And if one cannot show a practical, working, social order far beyond the ordinary, one must give in and admit that conflicts are inevitable.

Fukuden or Selfless Treasure

When one can prove in practical working this new life of infinite Fukuden, one lights a torch that shines through the darkness. We must not think it is only for a chosen few to live this new life. Anyone who steps resolutely forward with that lighted torch of Sange and selflessness will be able to go on step by step. At this point the devil of egoism and greed knows that he is almost certain to be defeated. At the very outset people should remind themselves that when they take up the torch of Fukuden and seek only purified wealth, this devil gets very frightened.

This devil is always close at hand and within oneself. It pervades one's mind and body in everyday life. To banish it is to enter upon a new life which is outwardly a life of Sange. Living this life all problems are solved, and one finds it possible to rebuild both lives and organizations without the presence of any disrupting element.

Illumined by this torch, intellectuality, emotion, and volition can exist fruitfully. All kinds of culture can flourish. A harmonious economic order is also possible. And paradise,[1] in actual fact, comes into being.

Now let us return to the practical side of Fukuden as purified wealth. When the devil of desire and egoism is overcome, the demand for things decreases and with it the demand for an increasing number of consumer goods — that is more than are ordinarily necessary. It may be good to construct new buildings, but it is equally necessary to extinguish the fire that destroys them as a dry grass field. Sange, penitence, is the means of extinguishing the fire of greed. In this sense it is truly positive.

It is our custom in Ittoen to say, 'Let us live with permission of Light, dependent on Fukuden'.

---

[1] Compare the 'Kingdom of Heaven' spoken of by Christ.　　　M.B.B.

Chapter 4

TAKUHATSU AND DEPENDENCE ON THE LAWS OF NATURE
(First Part)

You have asked me to tell you something about Takuhatsu. Those who know or have heard about the birth of this new life will understand that since it was born I have never made plans ahead and that my sole desire is to act according to the directions of Light. Therefore I am not in the least concerned about the future. From the point of view of common sense this life may seem very precarious. But on the contrary I would not be able to take a single step if I worried about the future, and I cannot change the course I laid down in the beginning when this new life was born. Let me take an example. As I have died to self, it follows that my wife and children must be left to the care of Light. For my own part, my task is to devote my life to those who come to me in the name of Light. In my previous life I could not serve others, not even those who followed me, because I used up my fallible human wisdom and little strength in supporting my family. It is true that a person so situated may make some gift or do some small service for others, but always within very strict limits lest he weaken his own economic position. If he has to keep up the position of his family he will need to set aside money limitlessly. It is also true that other people may give away certain moneys, but at the back of their minds is the fact that it will

86

ultimately be for their own benefit or at least for giving them a good name.

A business man must always be prepared to be confronted by rivals proportionate to his own status and ability, just as a strong fortress must be built when people expect to be confronted by strong enemies. And a millionaire must keep himself prepared to meet world-wide economic fluctuations. When a man has thus to guard his economic life it is not easy for him to give money from wholly unselfish motives.[1] I had no idea of these ultimate implications until my new way of life opened my eyes to the fact that 'a lantern offered by a poor person (to a temple) is of more value than a myriad lanterns offered by a wealthy person'.

There have always been some acts, even during the devastations of the World War, which aimed at creating peace. These acts are like salt that prevents total corruption. Also, the founders of the great religious movements did very humble acts with the same object. They went barefoot, prayed in the streets, washed the feet of their disciples, gave up the throne. They did not dream that these acts of theirs were laying the foundation of heroic deeds and mighty religious movements. People can never foresee the repercussions of little acts performed without the least thought of self. Thanks to Light, I could now see and understand these things.

It may seem strange to say that man should abandon his family. But when one is reborn into this new life, such abandonment really means giving them also new life. In my own district business men would sometimes apprentice their beloved sons to other masters who would train them by placing them to begin with in the very lowliest position. There is a saying that a lion throws its beloved cubs over a precipice. Abandoning one's family is like that. It is not giving them up but giving them new life. It means handing them over from the prejudiced love of a human being into the

[1] i.e. Christ's saying that it is easier for a camel to go through the eye of a needle than for a rich man to enter the Kingdom of Heaven.   M.B.B.

loving arms of Light. In this new life the whole family is revitalized and each member gives up his worry and anxiety, so that he can devote himself to helping others. In this new life there cannot be any thought of egoism or fame. Abandonment of self is the finding of the Whole. Thereafter the Takuhatsu or service to others is not the work of the individual but the work of Light. There is therefore no reason for feeling proud about it.

The new life is not negative. It does not need the making of any plans for the future, for we no longer have any anxiety about the future. We are not imprisoned by so called common sense. When we entrust our minds and bodies as well as our economic life to Light we see the activity of Mother Nature which passed unnoticed before. This is the natural state. But human beings sometimes seem to disturb this great construction of nature.

This new life is not guided by man but by another Power. At times we may have anxiety about it, but the less we try to shape it, the better and purer the result. It is life on a plane higher than that of man's artifices. It cannot be expressed in words and is difficult to understand. People say, 'You speak of acting according to nature, nonetheless you cannot get along in this world without taking thought'. If I reply, 'I think I can', the enquirer still will not comprehend and I can understand his feeling for I once lived in the same world as that in which he now lives. To the end it remains a matter that cannot be explained. This does not mean that at all times I am led by Light. Indeed, all too often I find myself resorting to my own petty devices. But when I do something led only by Light, I am astonished at how splendid is the result accomplished. I therefore have faith in the greatness, holiness and positiveness of this unperceivable Power.

The first necessity of this new life of dependence on Light was, I felt, to place myself in the humblest of positions because I was now supported by the faith and frugality of others. I wore the poorest clothes, and when my wife sent me some clothes I returned them saying, 'I am sorry I cannot accept what you have sent. If you want to protect me from the cold, please warm me with your faith. The thing I need most is the help of your understanding of my new way of life.' She sent me other things also but I returned them all because she could not understand. On looking back I feel great pity for her and what must have seemed my ungratefulness. But I could not have done otherwise, and retained my faith. A friend who once took me to Kyoto told me afterwards how embarrassed he was at walking with me dressed in such poor attire.

On another occasion, however, I did accept some clothes. I was looking after a sick brother of a certain friend. As I would not accept payment his sister saved out of her own allowance, enough to buy some new clothes for her brother, and from her brother's old clothes she made a short-sleeved kimono for me. She explained to me what she had done and I gladly accepted the garment. I wear it even now.

And talking of clothes there is another incident very much to the point.

An intimate friend of mine from childhood days had become a wealthy and successful business man. One day he invited me to the hotel in which I had stayed in my old life, and asked me why I did not enter the business world again. I said I did not want to. He thought my condition most pitiful. I thanked him for his solicitude but said I preferred to continue this new way of life. The following conversation took place.

He said, 'You seem to me to be very discouraged. But of course people do talk about the ups and downs of life.'

I replied, 'I do not know my future fate. I am however never in the least discouraged though I may at times be a little elated. I have complete confidence that I can carry through with my belief. I can't explain it very well, but I know that the basis of my new life is utterly dependable. I hope therefore you will cease worrying about me.'

'You mean that you have abandoned all things of this

world? Well, I think it is a pity for you to do so, but expect you will carry on with it since you feel attracted to this way.'

'Yes, perhaps you are right.'

The friend then continued a little diffidently. 'By the way, I've something I wanted to consult you about.'

'What is it?'

'I'm thinking of buying out a certain firm, but naturally I first want an investigation of its financial condition. I'm looking around for a man completely disinterested to undertake the enquiry, for the fewer associates I have the more money I shall make. You say you have given up all interest in money, so I need not be afraid you will try and snatch away my profits,' he added laughingly. 'Now will you undertake the work of investigating this firm's affairs for me? You say you will do anything people ask you to do, is that right?'

'No, I certainly do not want to make money nowadays, and I did say that I would do anything I was asked to do. So I suppose then I may as well undertake the work you ask.'

'Good! Thank you very much. This firm's business is near Daitokuji temple compound. Here is its balance sheet, but I want a personal investigation on the premises.'

'This is a little difficult. I may not take the part of either party. I do not want to make money. And I hope neither side will lose money by my doing this work. I am therefore afraid my investigation will not benefit you.'

'That's all right. I'll be glad if you will go to the place tomorrow, because I have already told the proprietor that I should be sending someone over tomorrow.'

'This is all a little sudden. However, I suppose I'll have to go.'

'I expect that your lounge suit is still at this hotel.'

'I don't know,' I replied, 'I did once deliver a suitcase and contents to this hotel as security for my expenses.'

'It does not matter if the lounge suit is yours or another's. I'll have one ready for you. Please wear it when you go to investigate the firm's affairs.'

I was a little embarrassed. The poor kind of dress I wore
was to me like clerical garb to a priest. I did not want to obey
my friend's request to put on the former type of clothes I
wore. I said, 'I am afraid I cannot do that. I have even returned
the clothes my wife sent me.'

'But if you went to the firm dressed as shabbily as you now
are, they would never let you inspect their books. The managing director of the company has just returned from France
after completing his education there.'

'It matters very little to me whether this man has been
educated in France or in America. The fact is that I cannot
comply with your request, for from my point of view it would
be wrong for me to do so.'

He pondered a little and then said with a grin, 'You said
that it was your task to do anything that was requested, didn't
you? Well, my request is that you put on the lounge suit! Isn't that so?'

'Well, er . . . '

I was cornered, and he again laughed. It is true that I had
said I must do anything requested. And the two requests
could not be separated, namely to bring the lounge suit over
there, and to put the hat on and go over there. On the other
hand, it was clear to me that I could not wear my former
lounge suit in my new life. But I could not bring forward an
adequate reason to explain why his deductions were incorrect,
even though spoken in jest.

I said, 'That is no more than a quibble.'

He beamed, self-satisfiedly triumphant. 'Yes, admittedly,
but you should answer me even if it be with another quibble.'

We both laughed. But I left him with an uncertain feeling
as to whether I could fully comply with his request or not.
Incidentally, I had at that time no home to which to return.
I walked to the gatekeeper's hut where I had been taking care
of a sick friend. As I walked I turned the matter over in my
mind and by the time I reached the hut I came to the conclusion that it was ridiculous to have been caught in my own

words, for I had no longer any will of my own. This new life had nothing to do with whether this friend purchased the firm or not. I forgot about the matter. Next morning I was sweeping up the grounds around the gate when the friend came along in a rickshaw, and greeted me cheerily,

'I was so happy I met you last night. I've already 'phoned the other party about you, and brought your lounge suit with me. I've made an appointment for you at 10 a.m. Please be there then.' With that he threw out the bundle of clothes and hurriedly went off in the rickshaw.

I was taken completely unawares. I said to myself, 'Why, I have not even agreed and now he has already 'phoned the other party and made an appointment. What *am* I to do?' Anyhow the problem of dressing is not settled. Does he really think it is possible for me to wear such a thing as this?'

He had already left me. It was an hour's walk to Daitokuji temple compound. There was little time to spare. If the director was recently returned from France he would be sure to be punctual. I peeped into the bundle and saw the lounge suit, shoes, hat, even a walking stick. I felt as squeamish as if I had been called upon suddenly to play the part of an actor. There was my family temple Koho-an in the Daitokuji temple compound; so if need be I could change my clothes there. With these thoughts I took up the bundle and walked towards Daitokuji with it hanging around my neck.

When I reached Daitokuji temple compound,[1] I immediately found the firm's office just in front of me. The thought came to me, 'I'll go in just as I am. I can't help it. It is not my choice. I am being led by Light. What I am doing may disappoint my friend, but the decision is beyond my power to alter.'

I shut my eyes, and then entered the office with a serious demeanour. On being asked what my business was, I wrote my name on a piece of paper, saying, 'Please give this to your

[1] There are twenty-two temples in this compound. The point is that Tenko San came upon the firm's office before the Koho-an Temple where he might have changed.   M.B.B.

master. He is supposed to have received a 'phone call a short time ago about my coming here.' The clerk went in a little uncertainly. Then the director, a handsome man, came out and looked around without noticing me. I went up to him. 'My name is Nishida,' I said. He was obviously very taken aback to see a man of such poor appearance, and with a rather contemptuous manner led me into a small room near the entrance.

'You are Mr Nishida, are you?' He spoke with a sour face.

I sent up a prayer to Light, and answered, 'You have good reason to be surprised at my appearance, I hope you will excuse me. I have a lounge suit, shoes, hat and stick in this bundle. But my strange behaviour came about inevitably. Would you let me tell you the whole story—for the sake of my friend who could never guess that this would happen.' I spoke seriously, and the director's face became gradually calmer, as though somewhat moved but still a little cautious. I told him how I had met my friend in that small room, and explained to him how in my new life I did not need to seek for my own profit any longer, and that I had no intention of looking exclusively to my friend's profit any more than to anyone else's, and finally that my new life demanded that I abandon all strife and struggle and that I must always do anything requested without remuneration.

After that I sat silent, praying in my heart, 'Oh God! There is no alternative.'

The director's mouth remained firmly shut for some time. Then he looked up and said, 'I've met many sorts of people. But this is the first time I've met such a man as you. I admit I've been impressed, and you have given me some ideas.' So saying, he called his colleague who was also a good-looking young man. They were both most understanding and took me into a fine drawing room. They then showed me the factory and finally took me into another fine room where they brought in two balance sheets, saying, 'Because of our respect for and reliance on your integrity, we place two balance sheets before you. The first is the official one. The second is the secret one by which you may judge the actual position of our firm and make what report you think fit. Thanks to your attitude we can for a while forget our studied calculations to show things in the best light. Some day in the future, we hope we shall have the opportunity of looking into your way of living. Frankly our own life and economic methods are not always pleasant.'

I was naturally surprised at the frank, open attitude of the director. There is a proverb that fear is greater than danger. But this result went much further than I had ever expected the proverb would take me. I had been genuinely depressed on the way to Daitokuji, but now I walked back joyfully.

When I met my friend again I told him the actual facts in all detail, and very seriously advised him not to be so grasping. He said, 'You ran quite a risk, didn't you?' But he was a man of talent and had a sure insight into how the matter would turn out. And that is the end of this story.[1]

When a man is humble and innocent and led by Light, things happen far beyond human power. Even in everyday life it is a well-known fact that one achieves a far better result if one does not strive for a thing. For example, if a man wants to digest his food properly, his wish to do so will disturb his digestion. Natural digestion takes place when one gives no thought to it, but leaves it to the working of nature.

In the famous Koho-an Temple in Daitokuji compound there are several rooms for the tea ceremony. In one of these there is a small framed writing in Chinese characters, Bo-sen. 'Bo' means 'forgetting', 'sen' a small instrument for the tea ceremony. Therefore Bo-sen means that one can carry out the tea ceremony properly only when one forgets the sen, the instru-

[1] I heard that the wealthy friend later became a leading financier, a member of the House of Lords, and director of an insurance company in pre-war days. In his late life he is said to have remarked, 'I was won over by my friend Tenko Nishida'. He asked Tenko San to officiate at his funeral.   M.O.

94

ment, and remembers only the cha, tea. The best shoes they say are those of which the wearer becomes unconscious. One becomes conscious of one's shoes when one has sore feet. Similarly when one becomes conscious of doing a deed it smacks of a sore mind, of hypocrisy, that is.

I have been surprised to hear that in some country districts women are often delivered of their babies without being attended by midwives. I also know of a doctor of massage who is a deep believer in nature-cure. He says that massage is not really necessary. It is only the means to give people faith in nature. He is very interested in the likeness of this new way of life with the principles of nature-cure. He himself used to suffer from consumption and was cured of it when massaging other people. Being asked the secret of his restoration to health, he replied, 'Just forget your illness'. This is the same thing as forgetting anxiety about life. The way of our new life is to commit ourselves to the power of Mother Nature and to refrain from hindering her in her work by trying to add our own tiny human power. Various names have been given to this. One is Rokuman Gyogen.[1] This was only a label given for convenience sake, and it did not have a good effect. I then called it 'moving with Formless Light'. But this, too, was merely a label, and I took it off. I have tried many other names, but none can express It. No words can ever explain It.

However, to return to the subject of Takuhatsu. This is a way of moving which means a new life, moving like the flowing of Light. I have no home so it does not matter in which house I work. The residents of that house thank me for my work because they treat the house as their possession. I accept their thanks courteously. But in fact I do not regard myself as having worked for them or for anything. I have worked only for Light. Sometimes people call it social service. It does not matter what you call it. As I have no home of my own, I am welcomed to the home I visit as if it were my own. Even if I had only a small hut as my own there would not be this

[1] See Glossary.   M.B.B.

welcome to theirs. When one's petty self vanishes the Whole becomes oneself. And strange as it may sound, in spite of being homeless one never starves; on the contrary one becomes healthier. Further, being continually thankful all day long, all one's actions are a form of service, and one is asked to go to many places and to do various types of work. We have come to call this action Takuhatsu. Zen monks and priests also do Takuhatsu; their form, which is to take their begging bags to people's houses, is different from ours, but the underlying idea is the same, dependence on Mother Nature, on the moving with Light. I did not learn about this from any Buddhist Scripture, nor from reading the Bible. I found it, as it were by accident, once I had died to self. So it can be called the offspring of Light.

Chapter 5

SANGE PSYCHIATRY AND DESIRE FOR POSSESSIONS
(Second Part)

About four years ago the owner of a large hotel in Kyoto entrusted Ittoen with the care of his son who had been in a mental hospital. His breakdown had been caused by the type of family tension only too frequent. Good conduct, however insignificant, yields good fruit; similarly bad conduct, although apparently trifling, can be the cause of disaster. When a family becomes prosperous its head, whose actions have been the cause of its prosperity, tends to dominate it, with the result that any evil he does has an effect on the other members without his being conscious of it.

This son was the one in this family to be affected and he suffered a mental and physical breakdown. The family was well-to-do and spared no expense to effect his cure. Their efforts were in vain, and they were at their wits' end when his sister, who had been intimate with Ittoen, asked us if we would take care of him. I put him in charge of a very sincere and devout member, and like those youths of whom I have already told you, his condition immediately began to improve.

I looked at the son through the circumstances of his family, and felt I could see the root cause of the trouble, as someone behind the scenes can see through a juggler's trick.

Generally speaking a family is unconscious of the evils its members are doing which are the cause of their troubles.

When one of them becomes ill the only thing they can think of to cure him is to send him to a psychiatric hospital. They assume money brings everything, and that therefore money will cure a mental illness. But such illnesses spring from an unsuspected source.

If the cause of the trouble lies with the head of the family, he too is a sick man. There is a saying that no man becomes crazy by himself.

One day the mother of the son came to Ittoen to thank us. She opened the conversation by saying, 'How is our mad boy getting along?' Such a greeting might not be considered amiss in ordinary life, but as I have said he was not mad. If he had been, we ourselves would have been responsible, and so would his mother. If I told his mother that if he was mad then she was also, she would not like it. However, I had no alternative. I did so, and added, 'It is not only you, but I also.' She was obviously surprised at my extravagant answer, but she was tactful and replied, 'It may be so. But in any case I am very grateful to you for taking care of my son, and I hope that you will soon find a cure.'

I went on, 'We also earnestly pray for his recovery, but at the same time we help by training ourselves, for we feel that we are responsible for his trouble.'

She then said, 'As far as I am concerned I cannot think that I have done wrong, though I am very worried about the matter. And, by the way, how much should I pay you?' Naturally her thoughts always turned to reward and payment. But of course Ittoen accepts no gift excepting purified Fukuden.[1]

I tried to explain to her that Ittoen cannot accept ordinary remuneration because we are fed by Light. It was hard to explain what is meant by being fed by Light. I told her that we repent of our own wrongdoing, and that the food of Ittoen's members consists of what has been offered to Light following a similar repentance by those who give the food.

[1] See Glossary and Chapter 3.

When people give food in this manner, I said, the members receive it back as a gift from Light.

She looked blank, 'I cannot see what you mean. But as my son is being taken care of, I would like you to accept at least enough to cover his actual expenses. You realize that I have paid quite a large sum of money for the period he was in hospital.'

'I realize your intentions are good, but although I am sorry to have to say it, this thought of yours that money governs the world may well be the cause of your son's sickness.'

'I do not follow you, but . . . ' the subject of the conversation was too difficult for her and she changed it.

She had supper with us that night; her son came to the table where she was sitting and she said to him, 'It is very good of Ittoen and we are very thankful to them, are we not?' The two were accustomed to costly meals and our poor fare must have seemed to them like prisoner's rations. I heard afterwards that she had hardly been able to swallow the food even with her eyes shut.[1]

The sick man got better and better each day. This, I am certain, was due to the sincere invocation of Light by the member who was caring for him. His sister was very grateful and one day she came to tell me so.

She said, 'Thank you for the kind talk you had with my mother the other day. But she was very puzzled because she couldn't understand you, and she felt uneasy because you would accept no payment, not even the wherewithal to cover my brother's expenses for board and lodging. Would you not

[1] Japanese food is made tasty by depending upon the eye to give it attractiveness and flavour. It is exquisitely served and decorated. Ittoen's food is served from large basins with no attempt at artistic decoration. Probably the lady would find it also necessary to eat some European food with her eyes shut. Meals at Ittoen are served at low tables about nine inches high as is the custom, but here the diners sit buttocks on heels on the hard board floor. The lady who was accustomed to kneel on soft cushions would therefore have had an added cause for discomfort.   M.B.B.

please at least take this much?' The sister had been the one who asked us to take care of her brother, and she was a sensible woman.

I said, 'I was sure that your mother did not understand what I tried to tell her. It was too difficult for her to see how I want to root out the cause of your brother's sickness, not merely administer a palliative, by having him live at Ittoen.'

She replied eagerly, 'Please do this. My mother would also be very happy if he could be basically cured. My family is at present very comfortable in all respects. Only one thing prevents our well-being and that is my brother's sickness.'

'What you say is right. But look a little more deeply and you will see the other side of the well-to-do state of your family. That other side is the unconscious wrong-doing, not only of your mother, but of most people who are unaware that all evils that exist are within themselves, and who therefore do not ceaselessly repent and strive to expiate these evils. This is the sickness which sooner or later shows itself, and your brother is one of its victims. Sickness does not come by chance. It has its root in happenings of days long past. We should be ceaselessly sorry for evil-doing which is always our own. Will you join us in invoking Light for this penitence?'

'Yes,' she replied, and then pondered a long time, before adding, 'Tell me what I must do before I can give to Ittoen.'

'That is a difficult question. But you can begin with an easy matter near to hand. You can start to reduce your own belongings and avoid asking your mother for more.'

'Yes, I see your idea.'

I went on, 'For you who are still young this may seem a most inconsiderate request — equal to saying that if you should put on a fashionable and expensive dress it might well be the cause of a great disaster. Yet this is exactly what I do say.'

'Wait a moment. Oh, Tenko San, I have suddenly realized that I *am* responsible for my brother's sickness!' Her way of talking changed for she had seen into the depths of her heart and knew her responsibility. There were tears in her eyes as she continued, 'Many years ago my brother was at a middle school in the province of Okayama Prefecture. One time when he was home on holiday I went to a party dressed in a gay and fashionable frock. At the end of the vacation he was most reluctant to return to school, and when our mother reproached him he said, "Why should I have to go back and study in a rural school where I have to clean the teachers' spittoons and do other menial work while my sister lives at home in luxury, eats elaborate meals, and goes here, there and everywhere dressed in gala attire? I won't go back. I want to go to a school in Kyoto." It was from this time that my brother degenerated. I think our manner of life was then and still is disturbing to my brother's studies. I was startled when I heard you say fashionable and expensive dress. The cause of my brother's sickness may rest with my whole family, but for me my brother's words hit home—"My sister goes here, there and everywhere dressed in gala attire." '

I was surprised and very, very happy to hear her unexpected confession. The sister's conscience was pure and she was expressing her sorrow and repentance to her brother's heart. In silence I bowed to Light.

Some days later the sister came to my wife with one of her kimonos which she had remade specially, saying, 'Please accept this. From now on I shall not bother about my clothes.'

My wife replied, 'I have already enough clothes. But in any case I could not accept such an expensive gift.'

But I broke in, 'It is given with a pure mind and you should accept it. In return give one of your own kimonos to some other person. Then all three will be purified by the gift.'

After that the sister's inner mind and outward behaviour basically changed. But the mother was too much immersed in the ways of the world to be affected. Although she remained disposed towards Ittoen friendlily, she belonged too much to the world to be sensible of her own errors. Nonetheless she was apparently a little uneasy, for she consulted a Buddhist priest. I gathered that the priest told her not to be upset about the matter. But such an easy-going attitude to error is dangerous.

The sister became more and more interested in Ittoen's way of life and the brother became better and better. The family often asked me to let them pay for his expenses. But this only made me reflect on my own failure. At last I asked them if one of our members might go to their house to render service in some manner. The mother was more bewildered than ever and said, 'But that would be too kind.' She still could not understand. I tried very earnestly to make the meaning of Sange and Takuhatsu clear to her. She became pious and anxious that there should be a good relationship between Ittoen and her family. But they continued to be wholly absorbed in the making of money. And without pondering over one's own shortcomings good cannot come from mere prosperity. There are far too many families reaching out after the same thing and the result is all manner of sickness. Then they go to a doctor to cure them and because they think gold is the governor of the world, they expect that all their troubles will be disposed of by money alone. Worse still, they do not hesitate to use any means to make money. Thus evil and wrong-doing accumulate.

Ittoen is not a hospital, nor is it a reformatory. All we seek is to take on our shoulders the burden of the wrong-doing of the world, and do what we can to expiate it.

The other day I was summoned to the Social Services Department of the City Council, and asked to enter Ittoen under whichever of certain headings was suitable: reformatory, employment agency, relief society, or various others. Ittoen has something of all of them, but it cannot be classified as any one.

I said to the officer, 'If you insist on classifying it, call it the business of Sange, penitence.'

The officer said, 'I am a little embarrassed to say so, but this is not among the classifications listed.'

No one seems to understand the prayerful thought that Ittoen constantly holds in mind.

The younger brother was at length completely cured. How often might families in similar distress be saved from ruin and sick persons cured if people would probe within their own hearts to find the cause of the failure and the source of the sickness. From the standpoint of Ittoen all of mankind is responsible for all sin and wrong-doing. Therefore money can never pay for the services of Ittoen. Nonetheless people think that everything can be gauged with the measuring rod of money. Apart from food, they think money can pay for a study undertaken at the risk of a man's life, for a woman's chastity, and even for a man's soul. Religion itself bows to money. And of course politics are governed by money. I merely state facts which everyone admits. I do not state that they are either right or wrong. Perhaps for those who have not found our new way of life, they may be unavoidable.

When I began my new life I died to the life of the ordinary world and entered a new world. All have implanted within them a longing to leave this ordinary world behind and find what is their native land, the world of Light. This is what is meant by Paradise or Heaven. I also call it Oneness or Nature. In that world one's attitude is completely altered and likewise one's behaviour. This is because one's life has been reorientated. As I said before, it is like waking up with a normal temperature after having had a high fever. There is then no longer need to worry about the livelihood of one's family, for one knows complete security. How I wish everyone would try it just as they would try an anti-fever medicine.

I do not say that money itself is wrong. What is wrong is the thought that everything can be bought with money and that money is therefore indispensable. From this thought grows the desire to occupy the territory of another country. What seems a small evil grows into this disastrous greed. The trouble with money is that it is the dominant outward expression of acquisitive greed, man's desire for possessions and yet more possessions. Therefore when I speak of money, I mean not only coins and notes and bank accounts, but desire for possessions. If a man could give up the thought that possessions are necessary, then most troubles would come to an end.

Some say that the ending of desire for possessions is not a moral problem but if we include under the term desire for possessions, the desire to monopolize somebody's love or the desire to dominate one's family, then we can see that it is a moral problem, and that to be rid of desire for possessions is to get rid of almost all the troubles of the world.

My new life proves the power of Light, and that one is completely safe so long only as one rids oneself of the desire for possessions. So I pray that people will study this new way of life, determine to experience it for themselves and feel penitence for their wrong attitude which is the cause of the agonies of the world. They will then understand why I cannot be happy when people offer to pay for our services in money. There is no need for us to be given money, nor is money necessary for the study of our new way of life. I want people to compare the ordinary way of life which cannot exist for a single day without desire for possessions with this new way which cannot exist without getting rid of the desire for possessions. I myself can compare the two because I have lived both lives. To dismiss a thing without trying it is not to study it. I therefore say again that I pray people will try our way of life for themselves.

Members of Ittoen should always hold in their hearts this background to their way of life and promptly do whatever they are requested to do. If offered remuneration, they should press their palms together prayerwise and pray that others will understand the meaning of Sange in their own lives. When doing Takuhatsu at a house members of Ittoen should not try to explain about Ittoen nor about Sange. They should not have even a passing thought that another's way of living is wrong. They should only pray in silence looking to Light.

Many of the families visited will understand the meaning of Ittoen and have the same prayer, but notwithstanding, they may offer some recompense. In this case we should accept their offer with a feeling of gratefulness, and so let Light shine through us that we may be a medium for Light to shine upon them.

There is a story of Sakyamuni which I like to remember. He was doing Takuhatsu in the Buddhist manner when he came to a riverside where a maidservant was washing rice. She dearly wanted to give him an offering, but she had nothing to give. She said, 'Will you accept as my offering a small portion of the water in which I have washed the rice? The rice belongs to my master, it does not belong to me.' Sakyamuni went down the flight of steps to the water and gladly accepted her offering, pressing his palms prayerwise as he did so. When he returned to the lecture hall he told his audience of the pureness of the offering given to him that day.

I, too, seek a pure heart, not any material thing. Originally material things did not belong to any particular person, they belonged to the Whole. Who then has the right to monopolize anything? Suppose a person claims that something is his because it has resulted from his labour. But who gave him the ability to labour? Was it through his own efforts that he grew to manhood? Another may assert that because of his own talent he was able to produce something unique. But who gave him the talent? There are people who have worked hard to give someone else a higher education. Other students obtain the wherewithal for their education from their family's estate, an estate which may have been amassed by exploiting the peasant farmers, whose children cannot therefore receive a higher education. Another student may say he has studied hard by himself; but whence did he obtain the healthy body which enabled him to study hard?

When we look into the matter more deeply, we find nobody can truly claim anything as his own possession. Nonetheless, almost all today claim the right of individual ownership.

A child is satisfied if he obtains what is necessary for the present moment. But as soon as he grows older he learns to want more than this. No one knows how this new attitude of mind begins, and yet all grown people doubt each other and struggle with each other. If a man wants to be freed from this state, the only way is for him to live a life that is secure even though penniless; then he has the proof. This is possible only when he has faith in the existence of the Buddha world or the Kingdom of Heaven. Some people say that every religion admits that this faith cannot be put into practice in actual life. This may seem a plausible contention but I think it is Satan who prompts it. I did not find the fallacy from reading any Scriptures, for I am not a learned man, I found it out from my own experience. In my old life I used to take the side of those who denied the religious teaching which inculcates unselfishness, and yet I had to admit that those who denied it themselves suffered from mental tensions. At the same time I used to say a little cynically that some religious teachers were the incarnation of acquisitive desire and should be a little less ardent in preaching against it.

Although it seemed beyond the power of religion to solve this problem, I did not cease trying to do so, because I saw that the desire for possessions obviously passes far beyond the individual for it leads to world-wide organizations, which in turn inevitably lead to world-wide destruction.

I was born with a disposition which cannot leave problems like this unsolved. Satan always takes advantage of a man's weakest spot, his fear of death. When at length my disposition to solve problems drove me beyond this weak spot, I discovered that I had found a fuller life, and at the same time the desire for possessions fell away from me.

In addition to Sakyamuni and Jesus Christ, we find many other founders of religions, who have testified both by their words and their conduct that security is found when possessive desire is relinquished. Their disciples who regard the words and acts of these saints as unattainable are unfaithful to the religion they profess. The mission of Ittoen is to testify to the truth that there is security without possession. When I first became penniless with nothing set aside for the morrow and I was ready to die, I found great joy and satisfaction. I saw then that everything belonged to the Whole, and that there could therefore be no question of increase or decrease no matter who owned things. The end of the folly of trying to monopolize anything gave me the feeling of being rich. Since then I do not think I have ever lost sight of Light. I have continued to live and so have the members of my family. All are supported by Light. Ittoen's members have increased and this little building has been given to us. Thousands of people have stayed here in order to find out something about Ittoen. The twenty members or thereabouts have never starved. They are all freed from the desire for possessions and are all giving service to others without concern for the future. What we have done during these ten years has been as it were, a work of Light, and we have done Takuhatsu supported by Light alone. The only remuneration we seek for our services is a prayer for the liberation of all men from their troubles.

There are many movements today that aim at ending the confusions of the world; communism and socialism are two. We do not belong to any of them, and we are neither for nor against any of them. Struggles between those possessing and those not possessing will go on endlessly. All we can do is to pray for the birth of a world in which people are content, not to struggle for themselves, but to give humbly and gratefully whatever they receive from God and be fostered by Light.[1]

Desire to take from others does not bring comfort, neither does fear of having things taken away. I want to root out both the desire to possess and the fear of being dispossessed. I seek to do this by the way of goodness alone without becoming mixed up in any struggle between classes. I feel I have found it. The way I have taken may seem insignificant but beginnings are always small. The fire that burns out a vast field

[1] Compare the prayer, 'Thy Kingdom come'.   M.B.B.

was small when it started. This greed for possessions springs from the insecurity of life. Would it not be wonderful if this small fire of our new way of life could spread to people who feel insecure and show them how safe are we who follow this new way? Then would this fire spread over all the world, this fire that is safe and causes no destruction.

If any of these movements which aim at reshaping society could show the possibility of reconstruction without injury to others, I should follow them. And similarly if world wars could produce a peaceful world, I would support the capitalist world which gives them birth. But neither give certainty of security, it is the Ittoen way that alone does so and I ask you all to study it seriously. I am not learned and I have many shortcomings, and I am growing old. I therefore plead with you to spread Light and destroy the darkness of the world.

However, to return to my main theme. Because we are secure and without desire for possessions, we may never receive anything unless the giver understands what is the very basis of Ittoen. If the giver does not do so, we must refuse his gift even though it means we have no food for the morrow. To go back to the story of this son we were asked to care for— in such a case we ask the members of his family to examine their own hearts, find their own shortcomings and repent of them. Unless we begin in this manner, there is no difference between Ittoen and an ordinary reformatory. But in asking the family to do this we of course do not list their faults or the faults of others. Instead we regard the trust given to us as a means for expiating our own sins, and we are grateful for the opportunity. Always it is the whole that must be reformed, not merely the individual. And it is not impossible for a whole people to become penitent for the sake of a single son.

Ittoen exists everywhere. This building is merely a gateway to Ittoen. Wherever he may live a man's sincere repentance and sorrow must have an influence upon the whole world. This is not a matter of theory but of observation. The right attitude of one affects the minds and bodies of all and thereby influences society. Contrarywise, when one person's life is out of joint, it too affects the whole. In this sense the individual is the Whole. Each member of Ittoen has his own task but he must at all times be aware that his mission is given from Light which is the Whole Itself.

Chapter 6

THE INWARD MEANING
OF ITTOEN
(Third Part)

'Come and try it for yourselves', would be the straightforward answer to those who ask 'What is Ittoen like?'

Ordinary things can be elucidated by means of question and answer, but this new life cannot be so explained because it belongs to another world. And yet this new world is under one's eyes as soon as one changes one's viewpoint. All scenes become different. Hell in the ordinary world becomes paradise when seen by the emancipated. The Buddhist teaching is perfectly reasonable which declares that this other world is billions of miles away and yet within a few feet of an awakened person.

Although this new life may not be comprehensible to those who live in the ordinary world, it is nonetheless precious to those who are actually living it. Some people say Ittoen is escapism. I prefer to say it means escape from the hell-like conditions to which these people have resigned themselves. But so far from escaping from the world, we work in the world's streets every day, do we not? Also, we can hardly be called recluses when we gladly listen to people's complaints whenever they ask us to do so. Other people say our way of life is negative, but in fact it is so positive that it can rebuild everything. Let us look at it from inside.

Firstly, no one who lives this life has his liberty curtailed. He renders service. not because he is compelled but because he likes to do so. Further, there are no grades or ranks. He does the lowliest work because he delights in doing it. He feels that there is nothing other than the sky that oppresses him and nothing that he oppresses other than the earth beneath his feet. This life is like an elevator which one moment is down in the basement and the next at the top. One day a member cleans the porch of a house, and the next he may be asked to give advice to the master or the mistress concerning family affairs. As he openly declares that in rendering service he is supported by Light alone, his wife and children do not ask him for money. Also he has no obligation to meet so-called social expenses such as presents when asked to weddings or funerals. In his former life, when he woke in the morning it was to think how he could earn more money that day, or how he could maintain his rights. In his new life, all he needs to ask is what sort of Takuhatsu he should do that day out of gratitude. His way of looking at things is wholly reversed. The meaning of the family is likewise changed for his family now consists of those who group together for the same way of living. If one of them deviates from this way of living, he is bound to part from the others even though they may be blood relatives.

Some may assert that this way of life goes against family ethics. But even in ordinary life there are few families all of whose members respect, believe in and love one another, even though on the surface they may appear to be living in harmony.[1] There was nothing very wrong about my family in my old life, but the members lived in a false position when compared with my family in this new life. In my present family no member seeks to have his own way. Instead he surrenders himself to Light. More than twenty people have come from both north and south of Japan to stay in this house. With the approval of the director in charge of this department anyone can become a member of Ittoen without even a letter of

---

[1] The Westerner must bear in mind the basic importance of the family in Japanese social ethics. M.B.B.

introduction, and with very rare exceptions all live on good terms with one another.

They are not given entertainment or salaries or pleasures. They go out to do menial work at other people's houses and may come back wearing second-hand worn-out wooden clogs. And yet they are happy and live in an atmosphere of ease as if their living were approved by Light. When a member makes progress in his self-discipline he comes to see how easily he might have settled all the troubles he had in his former life. He feels an ecstacy (*hoetsu*, bliss according to the truth). In his old life he could never wholeheartedly and gladly entertain a guest.[1] But now he feels like detaining even an unknown visitor merely for the pleasure of having him stay overnight.

Although I may look like the owner of this house, I do not feel so, and besides I am away from it most of the time. This house has many entrances but its doors are never locked, and from the street it looks like a roadside shrine. Visitors have asked me if it is not unsafe to leave it open. The big villas nearby have their doors securely locked, and when I come back late at night, I sometimes hear metal rattling apparently as a means to frighten burglars away. I thank these people for their good advice, but we have never given the matter a thought because we never have anything to steal.[2] When a person comes to Ittoen I always tell him he should bring as few things as possible lest they be stolen. But the truth is that one cannot see Light unless one comes here having nothing at all, and begins this new life with the gift of his first meal and nothing more. Thieves must be well aware that we have no anxiety because we have nothing for them to steal. However, we often tell two comical stories of thieves who forced their way in.

[1] Probably because of the close Japanese joint family life.   M.B.B.

[2] Of course Ittoen today has many things which might be stolen, typewriters and cameras for example. But its doors still remain unlocked. Over many years one member could remember thieves only once. He was in the kindergarten and some dolls were stolen.   M.B.B.

The Inward Meaning of Ittoen

Early one morning at the beginning of summer we found evidence that someone had got into the house after everyone had gone to sleep, and had left before dawn. One member heard the sound of the porch door being opened and the doors of the cupboard in which bedclothes were kept. But we could not discover anything that had been taken. Then, after the morning worship, we found an envelope on the altar with a signature on the reverse side. In it were notes to the value of ten thousand yen, and a letter which read, 'I have stayed overnight without your permission, and I am leaving before dawn. Please pardon my rudeness and accept my offering to Light.' We all laughed saying, 'So this was the person who stole into the house last night. We must be careful because if we are often forced to accept money like this, we shall be forgetting ourselves.' I afterwards heard that this man, Sekida, was a landowner of Kochi Prefecture, who was genuinely devout and had left home for a period of self-discipline.

The other thief was a woman. I wander from my subject a little but I must tell you about her for her story shows the fate of a family partly influenced by Ittoen, but also influenced by another religious sect not able to deal with practical affairs.

In those days, I sometimes went to a tea house[1] called Nakamuraya to do Takuhatsu. The mistress of this house was unusual. Through Light I had formed a friendship with her. I was quite at ease in her house. She had a younger sister and both were well educated. She prayed that her house might have a good destiny. It would always be a tea house, and although she herself might have retired she knew that if she

---

[1] A tea house serves many purposes. It is a restaurant, night club and hotel combined. Clients from the upper classes come to eat, drink, be entertained by Geisha girls, or stay the night. Geisha girls are not prostitutes. They come of good families and must be naturally talented as well as good looking. They are highly trained in various arts such as flower arrangement, tea ceremony, dancing and music. They must also be adept at entertaining and handling men. When fully trained a Geisha finds a patron, usually a wealthy business man, and becomes his mistress exclusively. She earns high wages, and only the wealthy can afford to have a Geisha party. M.O. & M.M.B.

did so, someone else would carry it on. As it had been left to her by her mother, she decided to keep it and endeavour to purify it by showing loving kindness to the scholars, politicians and business men who were her clients. She hoped that thereby the time would arrive when they, too, would embark on this new life. She never tried to make more than an ordinary livelihood. By the power of Light we can thus render service even while being engaged in such a business as this. She treated her clients with great consideration, and when her relatives said she ought to make more money, she merely smiled saying, 'That would be too good for me'.

On the evening of the National Funeral, she offered a sacred light before the altar, had me write the name of the Emperor[1] on the paper, and gathered her servants for worship also. I heard afterwards that she scolded a client who had come that night to disport himself, and that she refused to render him the service he expected. She was about forty years of age, and despite the nature of her business, she never used make-up on her face. She worked hard, never trying to make money, and lived very happily with her sister who was suffering from an incurable disease. Neither was attached either to life or death. Does not the proverb, 'A lovely lotus grows from the slime of the mud', apply in their case? I think so. I always feel a deep reverence for them.

Now one of their relatives, Mrs M., also wanted to run a tea house in the neighbourhood. My friend tried to dissuade her, but was silenced by the retort, 'Aren't you running such a tea house yourself?' So the sisters were obliged to help her. Mrs M.'s house was large, and required many people to do the work and order its business. My friend conferred with me about the possibility of getting some of Ittoen's members to help her.

As a result, two students of literature from college and several other young men went to Mrs M.'s house to clean it

---

[1] The Emperor is the symbol of the divine origin of the Japanese State.
M.B.

Whenever she met me she said, 'How much do I pay you for their services?' I replied, 'I was requested by the mistress of Nakamuraya to arrange for this service, so please see her about the matter.' When she did so, the mistress of Nakamuraya replied, 'Better than asking what you should pay for the young men's services, would be to enquire of Tenko San how to manage your business.' Following this Mrs M. several times said to me, 'Please tell me if you have any fault to find with me.' But I did not say anything. She was a supporter of a Zen temple and gave it considerable sums of money, entertained the chief priest and had him inscribe with Chinese characters a scroll which she hung in her room.

She prayed that because of her offerings her business would prosper even though she might be sometimes guilty of wrong conduct.

Priests of the Zen sect are fairly open-minded and I imagine they treated her courteously in the hope that she would be saved in the future by some chance happening. She could not, however, remain without worries, because she was always borrowing money and was not a good business woman. Presumably, too, she had a guilty conscience because Ittoen would accept no money for Takuhatsu that its members were doing in her house. She tried to compensate for this by making an offering of money (some of the borrowed money!) to the head temple. Zen priests do not mind the spirit in which the money is given and perhaps she assumed that her offerings would stand her in good stead in unforeseen circumstances.

Two young members of Ittoen, university students, who had been doing Takuhatsu by cleaning Mrs M.'s premises, sought me out one day and said, 'This house is no better than a house of assignation. We have been pointing out to each other that the cleaner we make it the more comfortable it becomes for its clients and the more attractive, with the result that the families of the clients become more and more distressed. Isn't doing Takuhatsu in this house therefore all wrong?'

'That is a very reasonable question,' I replied. 'What you say is true. But if Ittoen's members did not work there, someone else would do so. The mistress depends upon your working without pay because of her stinginess, and therefore her soul cannot be at ease. She will have something on her conscience that she would not have had if she had paid for the labour. Anyhow I feel it is the fate of this house to be cleaned by Ittoen's members. If we refuse to receive offerings unless she begins to see the error of her own self-righteousness, there may be a chance she will come to realize she is at fault. Let us trust all to God and render service without criticism whenever we are asked.'

We drank tea together and they agreed that this might be so.

If Ittoen had accepted recompense as the temple priests did, she would have felt perfectly at ease. The fact that we did not, left a problem on her conscience.

Two years later she died, perhaps from anxiety about the burden of her debts, caused partly because she ran the tea house on wrong lines and partly by depression. She left three young daughters.

On the night of her death footsteps were heard on the stairway of Ittoen leading from the dining room to the porch. Two members got up but could find nobody, though there was an eerie feeling in the altar room as though someone were there.

Next morning the mistress of Nakamuraya notified me of Mrs M.'s death. She came back from Osaka and members of Ittoen met her and kept mourning vigil[1] with her through the next night. Some of the women present spoke in whispers wondering if Mrs M.'s spirit might have gone to Ittoen just before she died to implore us to settle her debts and her family affairs, and care for her three children. They asked me if this was the case, and I readily said, 'I think it may be so'.

Despite her generous donations the head temple priest did nothing to help settle her family's difficulties. A soul becomes

[1] To help her departed spirit.   M.B.B.

purified at the time of death, and I think she felt she must go to Ittoen stealing in like a thief to ask us to help her. I was happy to respond to the request of the unseen one. I felt she looked to us because we had worked for her without payment. Afterwards one of her relatives settled her indebtedness and took one child, while the mistress of Nakamuraya took charge of the other two. And we of Ittoen were always there to assist and help with advice.

I have wandered from my main theme, the inward meaning of Ittoen. But Mrs M.'s funeral recalls it. People sometimes ask me how we manage about funerals and weddings at Ittoen, saying that neither can be solemnized without money; still less, they say, can the life of a married couple be catered for after marriage.

The answer is that we live in the present moment alone, and that this is the only moment that matters. Jesus Christ said, 'Take no thought for the morrow.' And Confucius said, 'If one can realize the truth in the morning, one will not fear to die in the evening.' I once went round Shikoku Island worshipping at the many temples that had been founded by Kobo, a famous Buddhist priest of ancient times. I was wearing a sedge hat on which I had written in Chinese characters, 'There exists neither east nor west, much less south and north'. I was inspired by Kobo's words, 'This present moment is equal to eternity and contains within it past, present and future.' In our new life we entrust all things to Light and never depend upon payment which has been made possible because of someone else's attachment to money. I have complete faith that everything necessary will be given and I do all things as the spirit moves me. I am not unconcerned about the future of the young people of our group even though they do not save money for marriage and are not even insured. But I have no anxiety, for this life has a more important aim than any of these things.

Up to date five weddings and two funerals have been celebrated. There have been no definite ceremonies, but none-

A New Road to Ancient Truth

theless they have been solemnized in a reverent and impressive manner. In one case the bridegroom, a bachelor of arts, was from Tokyo and the bride from Kyushu. By mutual consent they were married in the name of Light, both having been engaged in Takuhatsu until about two hours before the ceremony. The groom's father and the bride's step-brother came from long distances to attend the wedding. Congratulations, speeches and taking the oath were all carried out in a proper manner, but all the attendants wore simple clothing. Of course the newly-wedded couple made no preparation for a honeymoon, But the groom's father, who understood Ittoen life said, 'I hope you will permit me to invite the young couple to my birthplace.' I gladly consented. He was a landowner and a good landlord to his tenants.

Another couple married at Ittoen, left for a honeymoon on Shikoku Island doing Takuhatsu both there and at other places for fifty days.

We do not spend money on marriages as is usually done, and it is the same with funerals. When people say we should at least put by the wherewithal for a cremation, I reply pleasantly, if a member of our group died in the street, he would be treated at least as well as a deceased vagrant. Even though penniless the cremation expenses would be found by selling his books and clothes; his coffin would be borne to the crematorium on the shoulders of fellow members, and as an offering we could find some greenery from the mountains behind Ittoen.

Another objection made is that my sons are already grown up and able to support themselves. But how, these people ask, could a babe at the breast be brought up if its parents were doing Takuhatsu?

I should have liked to be able to testify to the power of Light by pointing to ten small children in my family, but I could not point even to one. However, on one occasion a pregnant woman (a distant relation) came to us for help, because she had no one else to turn to, and she was prepared to admit her own failures. The child then in her womb is now five years of age and in good health. Before its birth she did Takuhatsu in a large hospital, and the superintendent there told her she should come to Ittoen to be delivered of her baby. We regarded her Takuhatsu as the congratulation ceremony. We tried to stop people from giving toys and the like, partly to prevent the expenditure of money unnecessarily, and partly because we did not want to run the risk that the child should disturb others in their frugality. We gave it red flowers and green moss instead of playthings, and it soon learned to copy Ittoen members in sweeping and dusting the premises every morning.

I sometimes say to the mother, 'You cannot have impure and unkind thoughts any longer, for you have been permitted to rear a child who belongs to Ittoen, that is to Light. You should give up all grudge against your former husband,[1] and also all your self-righteousness. But remember above all, that the child does not belong to you, but to Light.

The mother goes out to do Takuhatsu, carrying the child on her back. It seems that offerings are given to it, as well as to the mother. That is to say gifts to the mother are no less because of the child. On the contrary the two are especially welcomed in families that have no children of their own. We teach the little one to feel gratitude to Light as well as to its mother. No mother should claim that she has reared her offspring; she may say she has suckled it at her breast, but it is merely the working of a law of nature that the milk flows from her breast. If her milk is scanty she should look within herself for her faults, her worries or her attachments. If she does this I am sure that the flow of milk will be restored.

I shall add one more story. A certain woman came several times to listen to my talks. She had a baby whose father was

[1] In those days it was as easy for a Japanese man to put away his wife as it was for a Jew in the days of Christ (Mark 10:4). It is fairly obvious that this woman was more sinned against than sinning, but this does not alter Tenko San's insistence that her only concern should be to give up her own self-righteousness.   M.B.B.

not disclosed, for the child was the offspring of adultery. Her elder sister was a good woman who believed in the Ittoen way of life and the unfortunate woman often came to her with her baby. Her parents and brother would not assume the care of her and her baby, and the elder sister although in good circumstances would not do so either. I heard that the two sisters wanted me to settle the difficulty. I recalled the story of Hakuin, a Buddhist priest who was falsely accused of being the father of a certain baby. The baby was handed to him, he accepted it without comment, took it in his arms and went a long way to get milk for it. It might be beyond my power to do what this great saint accomplished, but if I were actually asked by the sisters to take charge of the babe as a child of Light, I felt I would not shirk the responsibility. If I could not raise it, I should no longer be able to speak of the care and blessing of Light. I invoked Light silently as to what I should do if asked to care for the child.

The sisters had no idea of my decision when they eventually came and asked me. I at once took the baby and was going away with it in my arms, when the mother said, 'Couldn't I suckle it?'

I again silently invoked Light as to whether it was right for a mother who had been guilty of adultery to suckle the infant who was already a child of Light.

Then I said, 'Yes, you may provided you repent of your own wrong-doing and purify your mind and body.'

She said, 'I swear to do so, so please let me suckle it.'

And I said, 'You are permitted to do so.'

The sister who had been very upset by the other sister's misconduct was impressed by her sincere repentance and said, 'Tenko San, let me provide the clothes for the baby.'

I said, 'You may do so provided you are more frugal in your own manner of living, and never give it clothes that are new. Remember that the baby's temporary father is outwardly a beggar. A child entrusted to me does not require good clothes.'

The sisters shed tears, the baby cried for milk, was handed to the mother, and they took it away.

I admit that at first when I had not known how far I should have to go to get milk, for a moment I doubted the power of Light. But now Light had caused the two sisters to take care of the baby themselves, and further, I had also caused them to be conscious of their own errors instead of only looking at the errors of others. I was overwhelmed by the great mercy of Light. Because I had assumed the responsibility, the mother had escaped from what had seemed to her an impossible situation. Although the sisters could bring the baby to Ittoen any time they liked, nonetheless they reared it themselves and at the same time they disciplined themselves. They felt sorry to think of the little one living at Ittoen where everything is so plain and simple and I did not compel them to bring the child here. Sad to say it died at the age of ten, and I apologized to its spirit that I had not taken it to Ittoen altogether.

Chapter 7

EXPANSION OF THE SELF
(Fourth Part)

During the second year, if I remember rightly, when I was engaged in reclamation work at Hokkaido, I arranged for the cultivation of potatoes, not only for food but also for the manufacture of starch, for which we intended to pump water from the Yubari river. We hoped to sell the starch to Sapporo city. Owing to our inexperience we did not harvest the potatoes in time, the river became frozen before the organization of the pumping was in order and they were buried deep under the snow. I was told they would go rotten and be useless. I therefore went to consult Dr Nitobe[1] of the Agricultural College in Sapporo. To my worried enquiry, Dr Nitobe replied nonchalantly, 'Just leave them alone, then you will not make a loss.' I was considering only my own profit and loss and followed up with a silly question, 'Can I sell them even if they are rotten?' He replied smilingly, 'Perhaps you cannot, but if not they will serve as fertilizer.' I was deeply disappointed and left him saying to myself, 'So little does a scholar know of the ways of the world'.

About ten years later, that is after my new life was born, I suddenly remembered the doctor's words and they revealed a deep inner meaning.

[1] Dr Inazo Nitobe was a noted scholar married to an American Quaker; he was later secretary to the League of Nations. He wrote in English a book called *Bushido the Way of the Samurai or Japanese Knighthood* which was translated into Japanese as well as other languages. President Theodore Roosevelt was much impressed with it. M.O.

One of the remarkable things about the reclamation work
in Hokkaido was that for several years we needed no manure,
for the ground was covered deep with rotten leaves and potatoes. We therefore got a good harvest for nothing. My new
life showed me the arrogance of man's ingratitude in taking
a gift of nature as if it were the result of his own labour. I
realized we could live only by reason of a benevolence dating
back to remote antiquity, and that we ought to render service
in an inconspicuous manner out of simple gratitude. Therefore I am now very ashamed of my selfishness in those days
when I expected a good reward merely for sowing seeds and
covering them with earth. Many years later I called on Dr
Nitobe to renew his acquaintance as he passed through Kyoto
on his way back from Taiwan.

It is a law of nature that things are forever circulating
throughout time and space without ever increasing or
decreasing. I am always interested in watching how this
operates in human life. Provided that one's work is not treated
as something to be exchanged, one is never impoverished by
giving it wholeheartedly. This is illustrated by stories and
metaphors from the Bible and Buddhist scriptures. A wonderful law of life emerges from under one's eyes. Over and over
again I am filled with admiration for it.

Sixteen years ago, Professor Nakagiri of Waseda University called on me with a letter of introduction from Ryosen
Tsunajima.[1] I had only recently commenced my new life and
I was in a Tokyo hotel with three elderly ladies who had asked
me to act as their guide to Zenkoji Temple in Nagano Prefecture. I afterwards heard that Mr Tsunajima had said to Professor Nakagiri, 'A very peculiar man has come to Tokyo.
Would you like to see him?'

It was the first time I had been questioned by a university
professor, and I was very serious when I asked him what he
wanted with me.

[1] Both these men were well-known thinkers and writers in those days.
M.O.

He said, 'Have you a house?'

I replied, 'No, I haven't.'

'Then do you sleep in the open?'

'Well, I am always ready to do so, but so far I haven't had a chance, because there has always been a house where I have been asked to stay the night. I did, however, stay three days on the veranda of a shrine—that was the beginning of my new life.'

'I see. One more question. I hear you don't take payment for your work. Is that true?'

'Yes, it's true. I don't like taking twice over, and I am already given the means of living without payment for it.'

'But surely you must take some payment in the first instance in order to live.'

'No, at the very beginning of my new life I was fed without any condition being attached. Ever since I have made it a habit to work until I get hungry, and then I have always been asked to have food, after which I have gone on working on a full stomach.'

'And how is your family maintained?'

'It has been my hope that my wife and children would do the same as I have done. But so far they have not. But why is it that you are asking me these questions?'

'Because I was curious when I heard your story. Thomas Carlyle wrote, "Divide a number by zero and you get infinity." Now you have divided a house by zero and you have found a house everywhere. Carlyle also wrote, "If one could work for nothing one should be able to conquer the world." I think that the freedom that comes to you from working for nothing is very precious. I want to study it as an interesting phenomenon from which various questions arise.'

'Then I hope that you in turn will teach me various things, for I never attended even middle school.[1] So if you will give me frank advice, in return I will give you a straightforward account of our new life.'

[1] In fact Tenko San was well educated because he taught himself.   M.O.

Many years after that Professor Nakagiri went to hear a lecture by Dr Nitobe about Thomas Carlyle. When asked why he went, he said that he wanted to hear what the doctor would say about Carlyle's statement, 'Divide a number by zero and you yet infinity' and 'work for nothing'. Dr Nitobe said that though this might be a mathematical fact he did not think it applied in practical life. After the lecture, Professor Nakagiri went up to him saying, 'But I have just come from a man who does precisely this.'

'I know the man you mean. I have met him too,' replied the doctor.

Carlyle's statement may seem strange, and learned men may not think it possible to act upon it. But I am satisfied that it is not impossible. When I died to self, the statement became a reality. But it cannot become a reality for a person living an ordinary life with wife and family, therefore many people become anxious about me and accuse me of being a heretic. One man of culture said, 'Not from the most ancient times has any teacher taught and acted upon such an extreme doctrine.' I replied, 'If this is so it merely means that no one has recorded a practical example.'

When put into practice this statement means that one's house expands in breadth indefinitely and that when a man takes no payment all houses belong to him, and also all beautiful things within them. The opposite is shown in the owner of a house who, immediately he sees a fine scroll-painting hanging up, is not satisfied to enjoy it in a museum or some-one else's house. No, his enjoyment is at once spoilt by his greed to possess the treasure himself.

In the Zen temple compound of Daitokuji there is the small Koho-an temple. It is a National Treasure[1] and has a very lovely garden. I was on familiar terms with the chief priest of this temple and often visited it. In my former life I used to take the priest some present when I called. Although even

[1] A great many of Kyoto's temples are 'National Treasures' and their maintenance is subsidized by the Government. M.B.B.

then I was perfectly at ease in this temple, it was not like my own house. But in my new life matters were reversed. I used to sweep the garden and would take charge of the temple when the priest was absent, and I felt as if it were my own villa. In fact I was really more at ease in this temple than the priest himself. A friend once visited it when I was there. He said, 'You treat this place as if it was your own, but it isn't, is it?' He said this when he was about to sell his own house to adjust his business affairs.

One evening the priest called the monks (that is to say, the priests-in-training) and said, 'You must remember that from now on we offer food and other things to Tenko San when he comes here.'

'Yes, sir,' they replied.

Then he said to me, 'You have found your own philosophy of life, have you not? Wait a little and I think I shall follow in your footsteps.'

It is no wonder that offerings come to the one who gives service for nothing. The words of Jesus Christ, 'In my Father's house are many mansions', are no exaggeration, for one's house becomes expanded in breadth indefinitely. At the same time one can enjoy the temple's treasures[1] with a pure heart because one is free from all desire for possession. There is no responsibility for their safe-keeping, and the things one enjoys are watched over by others. In my previous life I used to pretend to be a man who did not want to possess everything he liked. But that was only pretence. Now it is actually realized.

Exclusive attachment to one's own sons likewise fades away in this new life, and instead those who come to me wishing to follow Light, also become sons and daughters. Perhaps it is claiming too much to say that I have no special love for my own sons, but it is not too much to say that if either of them should forsake the truth, I could no longer feel any kinship with him. I might feel pity for him, but he would have gone

[1] Usually priceless scroll paintings and wall screens.   M.B.B.

to live in a wholly different world. On the other hand, if a young man, abandoning his blood relations, comes to me for the sake of Light, he is my son and takes this way of life for his inheritance. In my former life, blood relationship was emphasized above all else, but in my new life it is the relationship with Light which alone matters. This statement of mine may seem unendurable. But it is a fact that blood relationship does not necessarily make people happy, for instead of gladdening each other, they are often worried about and discontented with each other.

In our new life Light joins together parent and child and forms a new combination. Instead of the usual arguments that spring from selfwill and exclusive affection, they are tied together by a purified love which embraces all. No longer must a parent follow a wrong way of living so as to leave an inheritance to the child, for the child, thanks to the support of Light, can live independently of parents and their property. I speak from my own experience, for I have been a very happy parent since I entered on my new life, and I now have two sons who are filial in the fullest sense of the word. So far as I can see, they have no grievances against me. They are well aware that I have not so much as a hut or a small piece of land to leave to them, but they are happy in our purified relationship. I hear that some of my relatives are so anxious about the future of my sons that they have offered good advice, but my sons seem to pay little attention to it. They depend not upon their parent but upon their parent's way of living. Only a person who has actually lived this new life can understand this.

Looked at outwardly, my sons may appear to be only day-labourers just as I am, but they are very different from ordinary day-labourers. Certain friends of my sons may have made a success in the world, but their success may merely lead to increasing the confusion of society, whereas my sons spend their days in rendering service to society, and I revere them for being the means of calming down excited people with whom they come into contact. They can do this because they have accumulated Fukuden or purified treasure. I encourage them in this, reminding them to devote their minds and bodies out of gratitude, and also reminding them that they have special opportunities for doing this because they have no obligation to care for their parents. My sons agree.

In the life of the world, when a son lies dying, the father in his fearful anxiety feels as if he were dying also. And similarly with the sons when the parents are dying. It is because both rely only on the transient body. But in our new life there are many brothers and sisters related not by blood but by mutual dependence on Light. When there are so many others there is not the same loneliness when one loses one's own son.

One of my sons is now seriously ill. I am not anxious about him. I have said to him, 'Return to Light with courage and thankfulness.'[1] To an outsider, my remark may appear cruel, but my son has expanded his self, as has his father. This would not have been possible in our former life.

And now let me tell you how a woman's self may be expanded in the same way. The relationship between husband and wife cannot be treated like that between parent and child. I have heard people remark, 'Tenko San may have solved the problem of social economy, but I wonder how he solves problems of sex.' They have been more hesitant in questioning me about this, and I sometimes wonder if it is right for me to speak about it openly. It is certainly not on my own account that I refrain from speaking openly, and yet I would not volunteer my opinion, and I now give it only to some extent.

Various types of women have been a source of tenderness to me, often, so to say, taking a wife's place during the ten years of single life until my present Hoki[2] was given to me through my new life.

One day shortly after becoming a homeless beggar, I was

[1] He died shortly afterwards. Return to Light is Ittoen's conception of death. M.O.

[2] Hoki means Bliss of Truth. It is taken from the Vimalakirti Sutra. It is the name given to the wife of a member of Ittoen. M.O.

7 Ittoen's First Home

8 A Gyooan Expedition for Toilet Cleaning

trudging over the Shijo bridge.[1] In my former life I had sometimes enjoyed the pleasures of a tea house. It was not a very
exciting pleasure for I was always turning over in my mind
the problems of human life. I knew some of the Geisha girls,
and I don't think they disliked me. This will show you that
during the later years of my former life I was acquainted with
the pleasures of Gion-machi,[2] the gay quarter of Kyoto. I was
then perfectly at ease when I passed through Gion-machi, and
some of the Geisha girls I knew would salute me as I passed.
But after I became a beggar-like figure I felt embarrassed as I
walked along that street.

Now, as I was crossing Shijo bridge, I met, hand-in-hand
with her mother, one of the Maiko[3] girls whom I had known
very well and with whom I used to play cards. She treated me
as her uncle and would ask me to buy dolls for her or tell her
an interesting story. When she saw my poverty-looking
figure, she loosed her mother's hand and ran away as quickly
as she could. A wave of self-pity swept over me, and for a
moment I wondered if I should give up this new life which no
one had forced me to adopt.

The thought passed, almost as soon as it arose, and I remembered that my determination had come about as a result of
long study and meditation and could not be shaken by an
incident like this. I hurried on, but still felt a little lonely. I
made my way towards the right of the gigantic gate of
Sammon of Chion-in Temple, and from under the stone steps
of Yasaka shrine I passed through to Maruyan park. And
there was my dear stone statue of the Goddess of Mercy (a
gift, I think, of the high priest of Kyokai) about three feet
high standing on a stone pedestal in the middle of the small
pond with its many lotuses. The pedestal is inscribed with a
Chinese poem of four lines which I remember even now. I had
once remarked to myself, 'This stone statue is far better than

[1] The main street of Kyoto passes over this many-spanned bridge.   M.O.
[2] Foreign visitors are taken to Gion-machi to see Geisha girls.   M.O.
[3] A Maiko is a Geisha in training, a training which begins before she
has finished her schooling.   M.B.B.

any Geisha.' Now the beauty and tenderness of her face took away my loneliness. There was a rock just right for me to lean against. I gazed at her face for a long time, and it became the source of a love which solaced me in my single life. It was the first time I felt at one with a Buddhist statue, and I was profoundly grateful to it.

About two years later in Kobe I was invited to a meeting of about twenty persons of various professions. After several topics had been discussed we took as the subject, 'A study of one's wife'. When it came to my turn to speak, this is what I said:

'I have now five kinds of wives.

There is a difference in the sympathy given by a man and given by a woman. The former makes me happy, but the latter has a tenderness that makes me more joyful. It may sound presumptuous to quote examples from the ancient saints, but Jesus Christ had such women friends, while for St Francis there was St Clare who gave him sympathy and understanding in his espousal of poverty. There may have been men disciples who were more faithful and ardent than these women, but a different kind of tenderness would have come from the women. This tenderness is not sex love, for it emanates equally well from an elderly woman or a kitchen maid[1] or even a baby-sitter. This tenderness is the purest love of all.

When I gather up the various kindnesses I have found in women, they form one fair personality. Someone may say the kitchen maid is an obstinate woman, though you say she is gentle. Another says, "I have trouble with my daughter's disobedience, though she talks convincingly when with you." Or a husband says, "My wife speaks gently only when she talks with you." And people in general say, "Tenko San has a habit of overpraising people." All these statements may be true. But suppose for ten hours I go around and each hour I win the

[1] The women from the so-called lower classes.   M.B.B.

sympathy of one woman, the result will be that I am served by a tender-hearted woman all day long. I have no knowledge of how these women behave during the remaining nine hours, but if each is pure in heart for one hour the result will be that, when ten such women are tied together, they form one woman who is pure all day long.

In many Buddhist paintings there is a celestial nymph lying on a cloud in the sky and playing her harp. For me she symbolizes my experiences in actual life. It may seem strange to say so, but in my new life I see a celestial nymph every day. It may also be a little improper to call them my wives, but at least I can say that through these women I find the sympathy of Light Itself.

The next kind of women are those who understand our way of life and try to follow it while still living as lay persons. I rely upon them, trust them, consult with them. They are a source of great assistance to me.

These two kinds of women have their husbands, or have had them or will have them in the future. But there is a third kind, those who are single and determined to devote themselves to Light alone. The nuns of the Franciscan Order belong to this class. When I am harassed or become weary it is this third kind who encourage and uphold me spiritually. The name Hoki, Bliss of Truth, is very suitable for these.

The fourth kind is the one who, with the benediction of Light, becomes my legal wife and is thereby distinguished from the others. She gives me more encouragement as a human being. By rights the women of the third and fourth classes ought to have exactly the same significance in treading with me the path of Light. There are times, however, when I feel that those with whom I have only a spiritual relationship are purer and more suited to the name of Hoki. I feel some impurity in my relationship with my one fixed wife, though nothing compared with the impurity of my relationship with my wife in my former life. In that life the love for a wife was fundamentally impure no matter how pure one might regard it, but the love for a wife in this new life is fundamentally pure no matter how impure it seems. So there is no harm in applying the term Hoki to both.

The fifth kind is my legally married wife who loves me very much, but we each live in a different world. So I have not yet found the fourth type of wife. But all the kinds of women I have spoken of have been a great comfort to me.[1] And I believe that every one of them is a child of the Goddess of Mercy. I may have said what seems over-pleasant. But I genuinely had the feelings I describe, and I did not have them in my former life.'

I was the last to speak on this theme and the talk then changed to a different subject. Now I have my fourth kind of wife, and by reason of her services I have been able to increase the efficiency of my Takuhatsu. There may have been some difference in the degree of sympathy and help given me by other women after I married my fixed wife, but I do not think there is any substantial change in the assistance they all give me in my mission.

There are many aspects of the problems arising from the relationship of the sexes that are worthy of consideration. Here I have spoken only of how the meaning of a wife may be expanded.

There is a wide difference in the outlook on society when it is seen from the standpoint of our life of Ittoen and the standpoint of the world. Our point of view (which includes this expansion of self) may be applied to politics, medicine, economics, art, and indeed every aspect of social life.

[1] This talk to the group of people in Kobe was given fifteen years before being retold to the group at Ittoen, that is, before Tenko San married a member of Ittoen.   M.B.B.

Chapter 8

ITTOEN AND THE ARTS

I feel very diffident about giving this talk because you are studying art and I cannot speak of what I do not know. I thought that not only would you find little interest in Ittoen's way of life, but that harm might come from disturbing your own way of thinking by my talking of what might sound strange to you. Therefore I suggested to Mr Mori, who introduced me to you, that it might be best to give a talk on ordinary ethics and morals which might be helpful to you in your studies. However, he said that those who would come here were serious-minded and would not be satisfied with only the second-best. They would come because they were deeply interested in the story of Rokuman Gyogan. 'Also,' he added, 'they know that despite my being an artist, I am your disciple. So please speak freely and hold nothing back. They are all eagerly looking forward to what you have to say.'

It seems therefore that I may be outspoken, and I think I'll tell you something of the relation between art and Ittoen's way of life. I don't know if what I call art corresponds with your own definition, but I shall tell you what Ittoen has been treating as art, and afterwards I hope that you will give me your candid criticism.

In the beginning, there were no artists in Ittoen but gradually some have come—painters, sculptors, writers and also others who were aspiring to become artists. I have listened to what they said, and through them, Ittoen has to some extent come into contact with the arts, and I have gradually learned to understand the nature of what is called art.

I am told that many people say Ittoen's life lacks the element of art and has no artistic sense. This may very well be correct because at the beginning I never thought about art. I started this new way of life because of the standstill I had come to in my former life, and naturally I used religious terminology. The term 'art' sounded strange to me. However, I have now come to see that this new life must have some connection with the arts because many artists have come to Ittoen and appreciated their taste of it.

A long time ago I did Takuhatsu at a villa owned by an old lady who intended to give it to her favourite grandson. It happened that at this time some of the fine tea-ceremony rooms had been rented to a wealthy man for the purpose of an art exhibition. A curio dealer dressed in an attractive kimono burned incense in the rooms and watered the gardens to make the surroundings pleasant. When all the preparations were complete the curio dealer came into the kitchen where I was with the old lady and her grandson, all of us dressed in ordinary clothes.

The dealer was smoking an expensive cigar and said proudly, 'Revered Madam, you may now come with your lad and view the fine articles displayed. The hanging scroll in the alcove is by Sanya[1] and is worth a huge sum. The six-folded screen is worth not much less and the carpet in the next room worth . . . ' and so on and so forth. Then, as if showing me a great favour, he added, 'You may come also and see the exhibition.' So I followed them all out.

The articles had indeed been very finely displayed, and not only the scroll and the screen but all of them were splendid exhibits.

When we returned to the kitchen the old lady said to her grandson with envy in her voice, 'One day you must become rich enough to buy such a great work of art as that scroll painting.'

The child was about eleven years old, and I had cherished

---

[1] Sanyo was a famous patriot and artist of ancient times.　　　　M.O.

great hope for his future. To me it was as if the grandmother had poured poison into the child's mouth. Nonetheless I might have remained silent had she not turned to me saying, 'Isn't that so, Tenko San?'

I looked at the child and replied in words that must have seemed to her abominable, 'How frightful it would be if you *were* to become such a man.'

The lady was shocked and opened her eyes wide as she asked, 'What on earth do you mean by that remark?'

I continued, 'You ought not to buy, let alone pay a huge sum of money for a picture which Sanyo once painted for the mere pleasure of painting, but I hope that you will become a great artist yourself so that people will want to buy what *you* have painted for pleasure. I hope that you will *not* become the mean type of man who boasts of being able to display such things. Rather your goodness should be such that, no matter how few your possessions, people will nonetheless gather around you.'

The old lady was speechless and the man with the huge cigar left for the exhibition rooms with an amazed look on his face.

I do not know how much the painting by Sanyo is worth as a work of art. I was not in the least interested. In my life of Takuhatsu there was a religious work of art of far greater attraction. By the way, I heard that the year after, the wealthy man suffered a great loss and had to sell his antiques by auction. Perhaps the same curio dealer acted as intermediary for the wealthy man who purchased them, and perhaps he is now exhibiting the same things in someone else's villa. When a man gets into business difficulties like this, Ittoen offers him a haven even though it has no costly curios.

This incident happened about thirteen or fourteen years ago. Six years afterwards, a young sculptor who had graduated from an arts college, came to Ittoen. He had been a brilliant student but had fallen a victim to drink. He had a son but was separated from his wife and was now dependent upon his uncle. It was the uncle who brought the young man to Ittoen saying that he would be responsible for his expenses. I thought it would not be possible for the young man to brace himself if he thought his expenses were being met by his uncle. I therefore said to the uncle, 'If you feel sorry and want to pay money because of leaving your nephew with us, you can make an offering to Light. But as far as Ittoen is concerned, we shall feed him in the name of Light so long as he observes the rules of Ittoen's life. He will never be cured of his bad habits unless he thinks he has been abandoned by his relative. I think it is necessary for him to work for some time without being paid for working. He will then be fed by Ittoen and learn to discipline himself.'

The uncle gladly agreed.

The young artist had to do routine work to which he was not accustomed, and he had to give up his favourite work as well as his drinking. He must have felt very frustrated and often he would come to me saying:

'If I have to work hard, I think I ought to work hard at some work of art. Art is as holy and sacred as religion, isn't it?'

I knew that if he were permitted to do what he called a work of art, it would mean the expenditure of money. Further, everyone said that if money were given him to meet his expenses he would spend most of it on drink. I therefore replied:

'You ought not to do any work of art until someone with a pure mind asks you to do so. Further, you may not ask anyone to buy what you have produced. A member of Ittoen never asks anyone for anything. Even when he merely sweeps a house he is happy to do so as a sort of Takuhatsu. However splendid a work of art may be, it cannot be of the highest value if it is not made in the natural course of things, or if it is sold because people have been asked to buy. I believe that you should continue with toilet cleaning or some other so-

called low work until the time comes when people respect you
to such an extent that they ask you to produce a work of art
for them. If, as you say, the object of art is to make people
happy, then the same result will be obtained if you do Takuhatsu, will it not?'

Despite his objections he patiently followed our way of
life, placed confidence in me and gently obeyed my instruc-
tions.

On his first Takuhatsu expedition he went to the house of
a doll-manufacturer in Fushimi to make models of dolls. When
the manufacturer offered us a fee for his work, the Toban
said, 'Do not bring money to us, but please pray for the
young man.' The manufacturer was deeply moved and the
young artist by reason of his abstinence from wine gradually
began to regain confidence in himself, while his Takuhatsu of
making dolls had a good influence on the family of the
manufacturer.

The head of the house came to us and said, 'Thanks to the
services of this young man, we have ourselves improved in
our work and I cannot do otherwise than offer some money
as a token of our appreciation. Will you please accept it, not
as payment but as an offering to Light'.

I did not know whether or not the dolls he made were
good, but I was happy to hear that the atmosphere of that
house had become peaceful and sober.

Some time after this I received another request. A certain
family having failed in its business, sold its house and moved
into a rented one. The family had a custom of holding a ceremony every year for the worship of the Jizo, the statue of the
guardian deity which stood in a shrine in the corner of their
garden. Now that they were in another house, they could not
follow their former custom and the mistress and grandmother
felt forsaken.

For this reason the master wanted to install a Jizo in a
shrine in their rented house and he came to me about the
matter, saying: 'We were very moved to hear that since

137

coming to Ittoen, Mr X (the artist) has become both serious-minded and sober. Would you let him sculpture for us a statue of a Jizo, and please tell me how much I should pay for this.' I replied 'Your request is very good and he will be glad to fulfil it. As a rule we do not accept payment for services. Instead of making a payment, I should like you to join with us in thought directed towards finding the cause of your business failure, and thereby rooting it out and restoring your fortunes. I pray that the statue which the young artist makes will strengthen your faith. Instead of paying for the work, try and find faith, for nothing sacred can be created when there exists the spirit of buying and selling.'

The artist worked hard day by day unaware of anything but the task in hand. Soon the statue was completed and moulded into a plaster cast. It was very pleasant to look at.

I installed the statue on our altar, and, together with other members of Ittoen, the artist and I chanted some Buddhist sutras. Then I prayed:

'Jizo San, please guard all mankind. I know that until the Buddha is reborn as Miroku to redeem all mankind you vowed to help guard us. Now a member of Ittoen, fed by pure offerings (to Light), has sculptured your figure. Please watch over both the artist who has made it, and those who will install it and preserve it in their home. Should those who preserve your statue prove unfaithful, please reprove them. If the artist should again fall into depravity, please fall into pieces, and if Ittoen members should fail to let Light shine in their midst, we pray that you will disappear altogether. In this manner please warn us all and so prevent our negligence.'

We ended the ceremony by chanting another short sutra, and then sent the statue to the man who had asked for it. I never knew what thoughts were in the mind of the maker of the statue or of the one who asked for it, nor could I judge the value as a work of art. I worshipped only Light and the Jizo who as its representative would grant my prayers. I prayed for the grace of Light, for I lay more emphasis on the people who preserve the statue than on the statue itself, for here is the true centre of things.

Again after some time, we were asked to care for an insane man who was in a mental hospital. Several members took it in turns to visit and look after him. When the artist's turn came, as well as caring for the sick man he made a fine Buddhist statue of Bensaiten for him. It was really good. But I still regarded the spirit in which he nursed the sick man as dearer than this work of art. He also made a statue of Hotei and coloured it. Being unable to buy paints he got the bark of a tree growing in the mountains behind Ittoen and made a dye from this. His action showed that he had re-dyed his mind also, for it meant that he had ceased wasting money. After a year or so, although he may have very occasionally run off the track in secret, for practical purposes, he was a completely reformed character.

There was a teacher of Konkokyo[1] called Masao Takahashi, who had found a new life, and like a member of Ittoen, he had started homeless. At this time he visited Ittoen, and, hearing about the artist, went into his disorderly workshop. He picked up three small figures which the artist had made, bowed slightly to them in worship and said, 'Please give me these'. He took them away with him.

A long time after this my wife and I visited the head temple of the Konkokyo sect in Otani. I called on Masao Takahashi at a small hillside hut which he used as his resting place when living a life of Roto or homelessness. There was nothing in the hut, no bedclothes, let alone a statue of a deity or hanging scroll for worship. When there is true and pure prayer there is no need for an idol. Besides the two of us, there were three others and we talked together until far into the night and then slept on a few blankets I had brought and spread out on

---

[1] For Konkokyo see *The New Religions of Japan* by Harry Thomsen, p. 69. Takahashi, now dead, was a prominent figure in that religious organization and was once its president. When young he had come to Ittoen to learn from Tenko San and hence his intimate acquaintance with him.   M.O.

the floor. I still have the pleasantest and purest memory of that night.

The next morning Masao Takahashi offered prayers, facing in a certain direction. I followed his eyes and saw an object that seemed vaguely familiar. Then I realized that it was one of the three little figures he had taken away from Ittoen. 'It is one of them, is it not?' I asked. 'Yes, it is.'

'And what became of the other two?'

'I gave one of them to Mr Y. in Hyogo Prefecture. He wanted to give up drink, and I told him that it had been made by a man who had learned to give up drink. He said, "Well then I shall certainly be able to do the same as the artist did." I heard later that he did in fact succeed in this. The second I gave to a man with the same problem, but I never heard what became of him. But this is the one I like best.'

'And why did you like this small thing the best?'

'I truly wanted to confess my own sins before God. I was deeply struck by the sincere humility of this man prostrating himself. Even now I worship it every morning.'

I am sure Mr Takahashi was sincere in his worship and that he was encouraged by this small figure of art. There is a vast difference between his type of prayer and that of a man who prays because he wants some material profit for selfish ends.

I was very moved by this talk and felt most grateful. If the artist had died at this moment, he would have died satisfied even though he had made only this one object, for he would know that it had received a far greater honour than it deserved through being worshipped by the sublime heart of this saintly friend.

I had thought there were two reasons why our revered friend had taken away the three little statues. The first was because of his interest in the works themselves, the second because of his sympathy with the self-discipline of the artist. The light that shines from a lofty personality gives life to a work of art—whether that light comes from the creator of the work, or from the one who receives it, is not material.

On my returning to Ittoen the artist was horrified to hear what had become of his little statues. I asked him why. 'I didn't make them for any such purpose. I blush with shame to think of what has happened to them. You know that I made the statue of Benzaiten in the sick room as a token of my gratitude for being able to nurse the sick man. When I was at a college of fine art in Tokyo, I had not cared kindly for my sick brother who was in hospital. I made my need to study my excuse, but even after graduation I still behaved badly. I wanted to nurse the man who was mentally sick so that I could make amends to my dead brother, and I also felt grateful to Ittoen's way of life that I had learned to have such understanding. The statue of Benzaiten was my token of thanks. But the third one was a plaything made in fun. One morning the insane man piled up the bedclothes and wrapped them in white sheets, then he thrust his head under the bundle. I sketched his figure because I was interested in his strange shape. I cannot stop blushing with shame to think this figure is actually worshipped by Takahashi.'

I almost burst out laughing. But his remark made me realize that in our Ittoen way we stress the need to make our actual lives works of art and that we respect as a work of art what has been made by a man whose life itself is artistic in the true sense of the word. However, you must teach me whether I am right or wrong in such an attitude to art.

The artist then went on to say, 'In my former life, whenever I created a work of art, except when I was deeply interested, I could not help thinking about making money. I always felt the pressure of life and before I started working I had to make a conscious effort to regain purity of effort. The works created under these conditions must always to some extent have been impure. But in this life of Ittoen there is no such pressure, and as I am now abstemious and fairly innocent of evil-doing, my work must have caught something of this spirit of Ittoen even though it may be otherwise insignificant.'

Even to me, an amateur, his works seemed to have a quality of purity about them. When I write a letter I notice that if there is any confusion in my mind, it reflects itself in the characters I write. Contrarywise, when my mind is tranquil I write clearly and easily. Similarly, an artist cannot conceal his inward feelings. His work will always reveal them. Thus a man's self is one with his work, and his work is one with him. If Ittoen's life has little of selfishness about it, then the man who has come into contact with it will produce work without thought of self. And if the atmosphere of Ittoen contributes to the peace of the world, then a work which springs from this life must also, in its turn, contribute to the peace of the world.

I have heard it said that art should be for art's sake alone and that it should completely discard ethics, neither condemning vice nor praising virtue. I think that is right, but I should not like to think that art could be the means of causing social confusion, or lead to depravity of mind, or stir up conflicts. Nature is basically peaceful and devoid of passion. Even though a raging tempest may sometimes fell trees to the ground, this is different from death caused by man's murderous intentions. A work of art which is in accord with nature and expresses nature, cannot lead a man's soul to evil. It soils the dignity of art to use it to lower moral values. If art is truly in accord with nature, it should lead a man's mind to Mother Nature, and it is self-evident that such art can be created only by one who is close to Mother Nature.

What is Mother Nature? That is not an easy question to answer. I think love or charity towards all beings is the child of Mother Nature. There is the saying, 'God is Love', and also 'Buddha is Charity'. I think it is necessary for an artist to be wholly altruistic in his body, his mind and his way of living. I do not profess to have a clear conception of what is meant by art, but a truly great work of art will not depend on a large canvas or costly paints, nor will it be confined to painting, sculpture or architecture.

Ittoen and the Arts

Once a person visited a calligrapher,[1] a good man for whom the visitor had great reverence, and asked him to write characters on a hanging scroll. The calligrapher had no time to write them, but also he had now become interested in the art of making straw sandals and had lost his interest in calligraphy. The visitor therefore took away a pair of straw sandals, hung them in his alcove and worshipped them every morning instead of the scroll with the beautiful characters which he had asked for. Straw sandals are necessities of life, but they can also be called works of art. If artists came closer to nature and gave up their desire to obtain as much money as possible from wealthy people, and if people ceased to regard only large works of art as artistic, then art would be simpler and closer to actual life. Both artists and people who seek for works of art, even though highly refined, are liable to be far too slavish to convention and a love of curios. Art would become actual life if people remembered that 'Silence is the crown of eloquence', or 'One returns to water after tasting all teas', or that 'Sakyamuni did not speak a single word during all his forty-nine years of teaching'.

There is no salvation where there is no suffering. Amida[2] appears only when people call for him. Mother Nature is herself a work of art, but some expressions of so-called art are no more than transient playthings of men. Of course I do not assert that actual life is the only art, but merely that everything can be made an art, including everyday life. From this point of view Ittoen's way of life is also an art.

It is understandable that some people should criticize Ittoen saying it lacks the arts and does not understand them. But before accepting such criticism it is necessary to define what is meant by the term 'art'.

[1] In China and Japan calligraphy is one of the fine arts. It in no way resembles our sign-writing. M.B.B.
[2] The Buddha Amida is the Buddha who relinquishes the bliss of Nirvana in order to save all mankind. He must not be confused with the Buddha Sakyamuni, the historical Buddha Gautama. M.B.B. & M.O.

A New Road to Ancient Truth

At one time the drama *A High Priest and his Disciple*[1] was staged under the auspices of Ittoen. Murata, the leading actor in the play said to me, 'Up to the present time our plays have been conventional and stylized. I want to overthrow these things. Stylized plays are like mummies which have been moulded into various forms dating back to ancient times. I want to invent a live drama which does not resort to conventional devices and slavish imitation, but is in touch with actual problems of real life. Then we can put our hearts and souls into the play.'

I was very interested in his ideas, and the presentation of the play carried them out. I had been concerned as to whether the performance would satisfy the audiences, for the scenery and setting of the Kyoto public hall were poor and the stage narrow. The audience sat entranced. Most impressive of all was the scene depicting Shinran's death-bed, when the only music played was a record of Beethoven's Ninth Symphony. The performance brought home to the audience the very heart of the play. Much to my surprise, Murata spoke on the stage in exactly the same manner as we speak to each other in everyday life. I recalled what he had said about overthrowing stylization. In a sense we are performing a play every day. In other words, life itself is a play.

There is an old saying that sculpture and architecture sometimes awaken faith. If this is true there may be some need to adorn our rooms and temples with paintings and sculptures.

[1] *A High Priest and his Disciple* was the story of Shinran, the well-known saint who founded the Jodo-Shinshu sect of Buddhism which has more devotees than any other sect in Japan. The character of Shinran was modelled on Tenko San and the disciple on Kyakuza Kurata, the author, who was a disciple of Tenko San and later became a noted dramatic critic. This drama was staged all over Japan and was one of the three best sellers at that time. The other two were Tenko San's *Life of Sange* and Toyohiko Kagawa's *Across the Dead Line*. In 1927 the *New York Times* wrote, 'Yet today the moral life of Japan is profoundly stirred by two great religious leaders, Messrs Tenko Nishida and Royahoko Kagawa, men whose speculations and life stories are the direct opposite of militant nationalism.' Murata was a famous actor and later chief director of the largest film company in Japan. M.O.

But when this is carried too far it is attended by evils and we should get rid of these outer forms. Shinran taught that even when not bowing before beautiful idols, people should live their lives constantly chanting the name of Amida; this was itself an overthrowing of idols. It was therefore appropriate that the chief actor of the drama *A High Priest and His Disciple* played his part with the object of overthrowing stylization and ancient forms. The performance ended successfully, thanks to the support it received from all quarters.

I should mention, however, that on the day before the first night of the performance there was some trouble among the actors, and as the sponsor of the play, I was a little concerned. I therefore said to them, 'I am told you are all sympathetic with the character of the saint Shinran, and you are trying to make the performance represent his spirit. Cannot you therefore each place yourselves in the position of Shinran and see things from his standpoint?'

By this I meant that they should try to bring the spirit of the hero of the drama into the problems of actual life. I do not know if they understood me, but they appeared to put up with any dissatisfaction they may have had with each other, and the performance went off smoothly. I am sure that this was because they really did understand the character and goodness of Shinran.

About two months after this I received a letter from Murata who was then in Tokyo. He reminded me of my saying to him, 'If you really want to end stylization in the theatrical world, why don't you regard your own life as a play?' and his reply, 'All the same I cannot think of my own life as "art".'

His letter went on to say, 'Since coming here our troupe has had many hardships from sickness and other troubles. Now I want to follow your way of living. When I was acting in the play as the disciple of Shinran who was modelled on you, I asked him various questions. Now as *your* disciple I want to consult *you* about my actual life. This drama is really serious.'

I was very interested and replied 'Come any time you like and let us perform a play that requires no tickets, and completely overthrows artificial stylization.'

Murata's drama *A High Priest and His Disciple* has been the result of the author's experiences in actual life and the actor who performed it came to Ittoen. Doesn't this mean that the arts and real life are intermixed? If an artist lives his own life naturally and truthfully, then his art will be genuine art. The technical skill is a small matter in comparison.

One's Takuhatsu may be merely the weeding of a garden or the massaging of someone's shoulder, but if one has entrusted one's soul to Light and is embraced by the charity of Mother Nature, then one's work is the equivalent of painting a picture of Dauinichi-Nyorai[1] on the sky, a painting which could not be sold for money. But others would appreciate it. And if one dedicated this appreciation to Light, one would be saved oneself. Is it not a great art to be able to save others?

Better than painting the sacred fire is baptism by sacred fire. Better than carving a statue of the Goddess of Mercy is doing the deeds of the Goddess of Mercy. An artist must live with his art the whole time he is creating it. If he does not, then the outward form will have no value. Jesus Christ on the cross is still living. Are not his words great art? The Awakened Sakyamuni is now living. Is not his begging great art?

I revere a painting by Giotti di Bondone, but far more do I revere the spirit which enabled him to paint it. I look up to a picture by Millet, but I am moved to tears by his life story. I lay far greater store on the character of these two persons than on their paintings. Is it not shallow to think that only their paintings convey their spirit? Finally, we may not overlook the spiritual sculptures and paintings that have been

[1] Dainichi-Nyorai is a Mahayana Buddhist representation of the cosmic Illuminating Spirit of the Buddha.   M.O.

produced by the good and the wise over all the ages. They are not made of earthly materials, but nonetheless they are great works of art, the greatest works of art.

I think it is dangerous to regard as art only what is expressed on paper or in stone. St Francis has nothing to be ashamed of because he was not a painter. And no one questions who is foremost, Kanzan or Sessyu.[1]

If one places the emphasis on the outward expression of art (rather than on the inner spirit of the artist) one cannot avoid being attached to money and money has no power to console a man's soul. If one's soul and life form an art in themselves there is no need for attachment to money, and one can talk with Christ and the Buddha and also save the souls of others. People cannot buy these things with money or authority.

I am afraid I have given a very long talk. Takuhatsu or Rokuman-Gyogan means beggar-like behaviour, then inevitably it seems to lack artistic good taste. However, I cannot help the opinions I have expressed. I am satisfied that there is a relationship between art and the life of man, and that a bright future lies before you if you are true to yourselves.

---

[1] Kanzan was a high priest of the Zen sect, and Sessyu a painter, both foremost in their own line in ancient Japan.   M.O.

Chapter 9

FAMILY RELATIONSHIPS

Sometimes when talking together men speak ill of women, with the result that women have grievances against them. But men can observe women only superficially; they cannot see the real truth about them.

In my new life I have come to realize that each should respect the other because each is supported by Light alone. When the man earns money and the woman spends it, it might seem as if the man were superior, and because of his ability to maintain his wife and children he may become proud. But in our time it often happens that the woman earns the money and supports her family, and that her sense of achievement may likewise express itself in her behaviour, for it is natural to feel proud of one's ability. But who has the right to assert that he or she feeds another? A woman is directly supported by Light because of her humility, and a child because of its innocence. It is not wrong to say a child should be grateful to its parents, but who can boast of feeding his or her child? A child needs food and is blessed by receiving it. Parents have sometimes received gifts because of their children and sometimes people weep because they have no children, but all should humbly admit that what they receive is from Light. I do not mean, of course, that a son should go against his parents because he owes all to Light rather than to them, but that parents and children alike should be humble towards Light. Because of this, in our new life, both husband and wife respect each other. I call my wife Hoki San (Bliss of Truth) because she believes in this path to truth and helps me in my Takuhatsu. This word 'Hoki' comes from the Vimalakirti Sutra which our members chant regularly. It may sound strange to call my wife 'San',[1] but she does not depend upon me and therefore is not my inferior.

I can picture your doubting how such an equal status of mutual respect can exist within a family, but that it is possible is shown by the fact that we live together in perfect harmony. The basis of this harmony is precisely this mutual respect for each other. The same principle is applied between parent and child. When I meet my eldest son of twenty-eight on the road, I greet him courteously as Yasutaro San and he in turn, greets me not as 'Father', but as 'Tenko San'. People tell me my son is like me. I say this is simply because he is my son. They continue, 'but it sounds very strange to hear you call him "San", and see how extremely courteous you are to each other.' I reply, 'Well, it is in this spirit that we have lived happily for fifteen years.'

And now let me tell you something about our home life.

Let us begin with education. When my son was thirteen, he dearly liked playing cards and became quite skilful. During the winter vacation he would go round the neighbourhood and sometimes not return home until morning.[2] My former wife was very worried and said to me, 'He comes back late every night, and takes no notice of my scolding. Will you please take him in hand and admonish him?'

I replied, 'Some time ago I might have done this, but I cannot do it now.'

She protested, 'But if we leave him to his own devices he will be ruined. I am desperately anxious.'

'I am anxious too,' I said, 'but I do not know what to do,

[1] In Japan it is usual to attach a term of respect such as San, Sama, or Kun, when addressing people. The only exception is when addressing one's inferior, e.g. one's wife, child or employee.   M.O.

[2] This incident must have taken place during the period when Tenko San was trying to find the solution to the problem of human relationships and before his fasting in the temple and hearing the baby cry.   M.O.

because I can't correct even my own errors. For all I know he also may be trying to reform himself. If I were not ashamed of my own wrong-doing I might find fault with our son, but as it is I simply cannot do this. I must first get rid of my own wrong-doing. I am in a very embarrassing position.'

My wife was not satisfied but she too had many errors in need of correction. If she really wanted to do the best for her son she would have reflected on her own faults and given up her addiction to tea-drinking, for example. But I was not the one to make this suggestion. The only conclusion that I came to was that before I could reprove others I must first become perfect myself.

However, I could not but be concerned about my son's bad habits. Then one day it happened that he came to me with a book and asked me to explain a certain passage as he was going to give a talk to some children of the neighbourhood. I asked him to sit down.

I told him how his mother had said I should reprove him for the bad habits he had formed. I went on, 'I cannot do as she asks because I am unable to change my own bad habits. But I admit that if I have to wait until I am perfect myself, then there is every reason to be very anxious about your future. I am not qualified to educate you. I am very sorry about this but it cannot be helped.'

My son remained silent but his face was sour.

I continued, 'If you were to say to me, "Please point out my faults even though you have faults yourself", then I should do as you asked to the best of my ability. If, however, you thought it unreasonable that I should reprove you because I have my own faults, I should not do so. But I should then ask you not to call me "Father" any more.' As I spoke I unconsciously put my hands on the floor to bow before him.[1]

My son seemed to be annoyed although he said nothing. Perhaps he had pierced my state of mind which may have

[1] The Western reader should remember that they were both sitting on the floor, buttocks on heels. M.B.B.

seemed strange but was also tender. The next moment he got up suddenly and ran away.

I said to myself, 'He is only a child after all.'

Next morning I found a letter on my desk addressed to me but bearing no signature. It read, 'Please pardon me and tell me about my faults even though you may have many of your own, and please let me call you "Father".'

Tears came to my eyes, I called my wife and said, 'Read this'.

She said, 'He was sobbing in his bed last night and seemed to be writing something, I suppose it was this.'

Since that time, although I have never spoken to my son in a voice demanding obedience, he has never disobeyed me. But I noticed that he was not so obedient to his mother. The difference arose because I prayed that Light would show me my faults, but my wife did not. Instead she scolded her son and depended upon her own human power. There is a vast difference between these attitudes. The first seeks to have one's child brought up by Light. The second tries to accomplish this by human power. Most parents think there is no other way but to scold a child. No religious teacher or educationalist ever suggests the possibility of a parent frankly acknowledging to his child his own errors, but my new life leads me to practise this.

Let me tell another story.

A child of one of my wife's relatives came dashing into a room and shut the door, holding it fast from inside. His friend came running after him and called to the boy's mother who was in the room,[1] 'Madam, your son, Kotaro, has slapped me on the head.' The mother came to Kotaro, who was holding the door fast from inside, and slapped *him* on *his* head.

Looking on as an outsider, I asked myself the question, 'Now what made Kotaro slap his friend? There must have been some reason, but only Light can properly judge which of

[1] As the panes in the doors are made of paper, the mother could easily hear what he said.   M.B.B.

the two children first put himself in the wrong. Of course it is not right to slap a person, but also it is not right to slap the one who slapped that person. If I, in turn, should slap the mistaken mother, then I also ought to be slapped by some other person, and so it would go on endlessly. When the child is in the womb it cannot learn that slapping is the way to punish people. What is the answer?'

So thinking, I said to the young mother, 'You slapped your son, didn't you?'

'Yes, I did.'

'What did he do?'

'The other child told me he slapped him.' She laughed with a strange look on her face as if she were feeling a little uneasy.

'But the wrong done is the same in both cases, isn't it?' I said.

'But there is no other way than to slap a child, is there? Do you know of any better way?'

'Yes, I think there is. You might have frankly acknowledged your son's wrong-doing by putting your hands on the floor and bowing to the other child, saying, "Please slap me on the head for having taught my child to conduct himself in such a wrong manner."'

The mother said, 'Yes, indeed, you are right, but I could never bring myself to do it.'

I replied, 'A child learns by example, and if you cannot act that way yourself neither will your son be able to do so.'

And that is the end of this story.

In the light of these two anecdotes, I think it is dangerous for anyone to scold a child unless he himself has attained the stature of God or Buddha. It is wrong to treat a child as of little account, and by so doing parents often injure their souls. If parents were wiser they would be beloved by all, even as children are, and also they would retain the innocent look of children. The Bible says, 'Whosoever shall not receive the Kingdom of God as a little child shall in nowise enter therein.'

When I bow before a statue of the Buddha I always notice

that its face seems to resemble a child's rather than an adult's. Parents whose faces bear the imprint of suspicion, doubt and insincerity, can learn many things from children. These adults were once children themselves. What made them worry so that they lost their former peaceful expression? Cause and effect follow one another endlessly like a twisted rope. In Buddhism this is called Karma, and the suffering that is caused by it may be said to be the work of the devil.

People call the birth of a baby a blessing, but it is also the means of bringing Karma into existence. In my new life I can see that this is hell on earth. In my previous life I did not see this, for I was lost in transient pleasures, which must always come to an end. When I saw the harmonious order of this new life, I realized why the Buddhist scriptures describe the life of the world as like living in a house that is on fire. It may be that not until after death can one be truly born into paradise, but it is not impossible to experience a heavenly world while still in the body. So let us make a start here and now to find this heavenly world. This may seem difficult, but it is not really so. There is a proverb, 'Though the road to Truth is easy to tread, there are few that tread it'. And Jesus Christ said 'My yoke is easy and my burden is light', and also 'Be not anxious for your life'.

We originally came from this heavenly world, and the only thing necessary to rediscover it, is not to fall into the hands of Satan whose work is to show forth a counterfeit of the real thing, to pretend a dream is reality, or nickel is platinum. Let us look Satan firmly in the face lest he take advantage of our weaknesses.

How does Satan[1] come into a human being's life? We should recognize him easily if he came with large ears, a gigantic split mouth and only one huge eye. But he does not come like that at all. He bewilders us by coming like an angel

[1] It is interesting that Tenko San personifies the evil forces as Satan or the Devil, but hardly ever attempts to personify Light. This is appropriate, for the dark forces spring from egoism and the bright forces from the Oneness of all, which is impersonal.   M.B.B.

in quite a friendly manner. Behind this friendly mask it is difficult to discern Satan, and even clever and awakened people are sometimes duped by his cunning.

The World War of 1914-1918 was the frightful mischief of Satan. At one stroke he upset all the prayers of the religious and the well thought out plans of the clever to subjugate him. I am always amazed at his subtle tricks which kill innumerable people struggling to live, and set off disastrous bombs right under the noses of the scientists with their marvellous inventions.

These cunning tricks he smuggles into all strata of society, including presumably women's societies like this. Indeed, they are secreted even in my own mind for they made me come here with only the pretext of your invitation. At this very moment Satan makes me desire to speak effectively. Even my endeavour to talk without injury to anyone may be the work of Satan. As he comes into our lives so artfully, we cannot of ourselves hope to be a match for him. Let me give you a concrete example.

An honest man once borrowed money. Then something happened so that he could not repay it. The creditor pressed him. His daughter, unable to look on with indifference, sold herself to the proprietor of a brothel. The honourable father[1] would never have asked his daughter to do this, and the daughter herself seems to have been a girl of great tenderness and good sense, and utterly unlike those who sell themselves for luxuries or pleasures. Was it not pitiful that, despite her own reluctance, for the sake of filial devotion and to save her family from collapse and her brother from being taken from school, she should have done what she did?

Afterwards it happened that the son of that merciless moneylender fell in love with her. Love is blind and is influenced by neither affection nor duty. Despite his father's

---

[1] In former times a woman's chastity was often bartered for large sums of money. The transaction was called selling a woman. The practice was only abolished after tremendous efforts.　　　　M.O.

admonitions the son ran through his father's money and, after his death, spent all to liberate the girl. Afterwards they lived together in harmony and poverty.

Now let us examine this story and see how Satan played his part. Why could not the young couple so suited to each other, have married without worrying their parents or injuring their families? First, see the subtle artifice of Satan in urging upon the creditor the necessity for asserting his rights, and then making the girl think it was obligatory to trade her chastity for money, and finally causing the manager of the brothel to refuse to allow the young people to marry unless he was paid so much money that the young man's family became bankrupt. In the end Satan had succeeded in causing all these people to worry so much about making a livelihood and to struggle so desperately that the result was the downfall of all of them.

You must not delude yourselves into thinking that such a case occurs very seldom. It may be true that it is rare for a moneylender's son to fall in love with his debtor's daughter, but each incident of that story is a common happening.

And now let us look at these circumstances in the light of our new life, and see how differently things work out. First the debtor delivers all he has to the creditor, and if it is not enough he offers his services also, and his good daughter works at the same house as a maidservant. I do not think that any creditor would ask for more than this. On the contrary there have been cases where creditors have been so impressed that they themselves have come to see life from Ittoen's standpoint. Then if the son of the moneylender and the good daughter fell in love with each other they could have lived together happily without having anything to do with brothels.

Although it is not wrong to think one must earn money, protect the reputation of one's family, and be dutiful to one's parents, nonetheless Satan always takes advantage of these thoughts to steal in unawares. Only when people follow

Ittoen's way of life can Satan find no way to enter. The Bible teaches us not to claim our rights.[1] For you who are housewives and therefore only consumers and not producers, the exercise of your rights may not appear so important. But your husbands will certainly have very strong ideas indeed about the need for asserting their rights, thinking this is necessary for the sake of their families.

To fulfil one's duty to one's family is important, but to give to it more than one possesses is to go against natural law. People are prone both to assert their rights and to evade their duties or, in order to perform their duties, to go against nature's laws. In such an environment even you who are consumers only are liable to be deceived by the cunning tricks of Satan, who is always lurking in your house and may bring ruin on your family before you are even aware of his presence.

Now, how about trying to take Ittoen's way of life into your homes? Picture a member of Ittoen coming into your house. If you have a maidservant he asks her to let him help in some menial work. Leave him to follow his own way. He may be educated or uneducated, a priest or a clergyman, the son of a rich man or a poor man, or even one who has been a delinquent. When people are members of Ittoen, they are all brothers and on intimate terms with each other in the name of Takuhatsu (humble service) and Sange (penitence). They regard themselves as responsible for all the ills of mankind and, instead of living selfishly only in their own homes they are ready to render service in the homes of others, confessing and thereby seeking to expiate the ills for which they feel responsible. They do not think there is any special virtue in what they do, but they are happy and at ease in doing it. If they are clever they may explain the matter to their satisfaction. If they are religious they may do it because of their faith. If they have been delinquents, they may find it the means of their reformation. Whatever the reason, each one

[1] Presumably Tenko San refers to Christ saying that if a man asks you for your coat, you must give him your cloak also.   M.O.

feels as if he has been pardoned and, however poor and feeble he may be, that he has been enriched by some unseen Power. Cleaning a house in this state of mind, it is natural to give thanks to Light when he is given a meal or after taking a bath before returning to Ittoen. He does not need wages or appreciation.

This is the attitude of mind of Ittoen's members, and you too can adopt the same attitude and by means of it thrust Satan from your house. Satan, who cannot be beaten by any other method, is easily defeated by Light. He is powerless against a person who sincerely admits his wrong-doing. But remember that one must continue to acknowledge one's own error even though after many years the heart of the other still fails to melt. My own way is to go on to my very last breath, to go on like this and not resisting the other. Let us determine as long as we live to go on acknowledging our own self-centredness and continue doing this despite the machinations of Satan. If one does this, one's own soul is raised up or resurrected and the troubles of one's family are solved. Beginning with one's immediate surroundings, Light of an awakened one spreads in all directions and exercises a tremendous influence. The woman who founded Tenrikyo,[1] which now has five million adherents, was such a one. She completely died to self. She entrusted her house and children and her own soul to God.

Because this acknowledgement of wrong-doing is directed towards oneself and not to others, anyone can do it. When Light is in control there is no question of greater or lesser ability—a maidservant, a son, a daughter or a mother-in-law, all are equal before Light. The only thing necessary is to die to self and thereby to defeat Satan through the power of Light.

Nothing is nobler or more precious than an awakened soul. Rags worn by an awakened one are superior to a gorgeous dress worn by a wealthy woman not awakened. Does the

[1] The largest of the new religions of Japan.　　　　　　M.O.

present-day family see the value of an awakened soul? If the members of a family are dissatisfied or worried, or if they fear death, it shows that they are forgetting their own souls. And when they do not realize that they would be safe under the direction of Light, Satan takes advantage of all their weak points. To acknowledge frankly one's own shortcomings to another brings mutual respect. When we respect others there is equality even though we do not go out of our way to assert our rights.

The *Saddharma Pundarika Sutra* tells of a Bodhisattva called Jo-Fugyo (One-Who-Never-Makes-Light-of-a-Person). He bows down before everyone no matter how he may be persecuted by them. A woman is given no weapon nobler than this. It is not cowardly or servile. On the contrary it will calm even one who angrily shakes his fist. It does not mean winning people by fair words, but worshipping Light that resides in the heart of all. I do not say anything against the movements for women's rights in other parts of the world, but I do not think that ideas imported from foreign countries are always best for us here. I look forward rather to a sacred movement inspired by Light and making for the harmony of the whole.

Satan is liable to lurk at the heart of all organized movements. The best movement is therefore that of minding only one's own step. Of course, support of organized movements is necessary in an organized society such as exists today, but the method of supporting them is very important. A broken cup must be mended, but it is better not to let it get broken. Blindly seeking to mend it may cause it to break into still more pieces. This means that it is first essential to get rid of the traps which Satan places all around us, and to do this we must look first of all to our own steps. I must, for example, be careful how I speak at this meeting, remembering that my wife and other members of Ittoen are doing Takuhatsu in the way I have explained. It is not true eloquence to speak haltingly as I do now, but to do the work for which one is fitted.

I do hope that you who are members of this Women's Society, can see the point I have tried to make and will avoid being caught in Satan's traps. Remember that we may learn through quite unexpected actions. Jesus Christ washed the feet of his disciples; a thoughtful mistress may repair the clogs of her maid.

Please pardon me for my plain speaking.

Chapter 10

THE POWER OF SANGE

About ten years ago the little building called Ittoen was moved from Kyoto to the inner part of Kosenrin. It is now occupied by many of the young unmarried men, but the polished step of its porch reminds the older members of the long history of their Ittoen life.

A week before the end of 1947, I gathered together the young men who were living there. A series of thefts had been taking place for some time and these had culminated in someone setting fire to a paper-covered sliding door. Who the culprit was no one knew and I felt a great sense of responsibility. I now determined to get to the bottom of this affair.

I would have made my enquiry earlier but I had been elected a member of the House of Councillors, and the sessions of the Diet had kept me fully occupied. But now the end of the year was at hand and I felt that I could not greet the New Year, the seventy-seventh for me and the seventieth for my wife, without discovering the thief and finding a way to help him. Further, I knew that I was responsible to Light if I failed to resolve this evil. Thus it was that a further burden was added to my work at the year's end.

It was possible, of course, that the criminal might be an outsider but, after comparing various reports, it seemed more likely that he was one of our community. Before talking to the young men that evening I had not referred to the matter publicly. I now spoke to them very sadly.

'As you know I have been keeping silence in the Diet ever

since I was elected. My reason has been that although the members were preaching increase in production, austerity and the like, they did not put these things into practice themselves and refused even to listen to what I could tell them. I invited some whom I knew to come to Ittoen and see for themselves how we put these things into practice in daily life, but none came.

And now, to my great embarrassment, we have been losing articles in our community. How shocking it would have been if some of the members had accepted my invitation and the visitors' shoes had been stolen while they were here! I cannot celebrate the New Year unless I find out whether the offender is an outsider or one of our own people. I am, of course, the one finally responsible in this matter, but the Toban of Ittoen House and his wife have also been invoking Light, and I now ask you all to join with us in our prayers.'

A committee of four was appointed to discuss how the young men should deal with the situation by self-discipline. I then spoke again.

'There are two persons who know perfectly well who the criminal is.'

I looked around at the young men sitting side by side. There was complete silence. I continued.

'The one is Light and the other is the criminal himself.'

Having said this I invoked Light, and there flashed upon me a feeling that Tomita, a young medical student, was the thief. He had been repatriated from Manchuria where he had been a member of the local Ittoen branch, and he had come to us. Although I had this flash of intuition, I had no thought of sitting in judgement on him.

Every morning after that my talk referred to the need for penitence both as regards myself and the young men. 'A theft,' I said, 'is not limited to material goods. We must frankly acknowledge *all* our shortcomings. If a member of our Agricultural Department were to put a sweet potato in his pocket on the way home from the farm, this would be a theft.

And if a man should be idle for even a short time during working hours, this would be a theft of time. With this attitude of mind we should examine all our errors.'

Each day I continued in this manner, but always without blaming anyone, and I also reminded them of the essence of the Rokuman Gyogan prayer,[1] chanted every morning in the worship hall, that the root of all evil lies in our own self-centredness.

Then one after another, the young men began to acknowledge that they had been guilty of theft. The first was a deaf and dumb lad of sixteen who wrote a note to the Toban saying that he had taken a can of red beans, and finished, 'I cannot eat the remaining beans.' The next was a youth who said, 'I confess to Light that I have idled away my time.' Another said, 'I confess that once I exchanged some saké (rice wine), which had been rationed to me by the Government, for a book that I wanted very badly. I now realize that this was an act of illegal disposal.' These young men had listened to their inner voices and were moved to frank acknowledgement of their errors. It was with deep feeling that I reported these confessions at our next morning worship.

Nonetheless the criminal himself was not among those who had confessed. At the morning worship on December 30th, I shut my eyes, saying to myself, 'Tomorrow is the last day of the year. If the offender does not stand forth, I . . . ' I felt almost suffocated as I wondered what I should do. For me it was a matter of overwhelming importance and I felt urged from my inmost heart to make some grave decision.

At the beginning of my new life, I had petitioned Light that I might never be the cause of conflict, or, in the words of the Bible, that I should turn the other cheek, or as the *Saddharma Pundarika Sutra* puts it, that I should never make light of others. Those from whom the articles had been stolen made no complaint because in our life of Sange we always take the guilt upon ourselves. Therefore no one in this community

[1] See translation in Introduction.   M.B.B.

would want to find another guilty. However, the orderly running of the life of the village would no longer be possible if this unprecedented trouble should be left unchecked.

At the end of that morning's worship, ten of the elders bowed to Light in the Muendo Hall, the sacred place where a light is always burning. They said to me, 'We are deeply sorry to have worried you so much, and we have agreed to fast today as a confession of our guilt.' I thanked them but said that they should not do this. Nonetheless they persisted in their determination and my wife and I joined them in their fast.

Then about three in the afternoon, a young man with a pale face came into my room and bowed to me. He put his left hand into his bosom and held it outside with a blood-stained right hand. It was Tomita, and I realized that my premonition had been right. He had deliberately cut one of his fingers. I nodded to him. I had no desire to blame him. On the contrary I felt more inclined to praise him.

I said, 'Yes, I understand. Tell no one about the matter. Merely say you have been hurt. Rest quietly in your room and I will arrange to have your food brought to you. But come and hear what I have to say at the morning service tomorrow. Do you understand?'

The next morning I gave my last talk of the year.

Partly because of their fast, those who came fell into a deep silence when the sutra chanting ended. Tomita sat upright in his usual place. I was serenely peaceful as I gave them my thought for the close of the year. I then added, 'The fasting of members has been a wonderful kind of worship. It has made you all examine your own conscience and take the burden of all wrong-doing upon yourselves. I am very happy. Last night I asked you to end your fast. And now you can set your minds at rest. The criminal has made himself known.'

Everyone looked at me intently. I shut my eyes and continued, 'The criminal was myself.'

An even deeper silence fell. I ended 'Please be easy in your minds and make your preparations for greeting the New Year. Thank you.'

The truth of the matter was probably not yet known to everyone, but they all accepted my reassurance: 'Set your minds at rest'. They left the Reido Hall and Tomita went back to his room. Thus we could joyfully greet my own seventy-seventh and my wife's seventieth New Year and enjoy the three holidays. That New Year seemed to herald a great movement of Light through the sacred swastika[1] of Buddhism and the sacred cross of Christianity.

On the fourth day of January after conferring with a few of the older members, I advised Tomita to deliver himself up to the police. And it was only then that everyone knew what had happened.

From this time matters were managed formally by the police. Tomita went from the police box to the police station house, and thence from the prosecutor's office to the detention house. The public was not conversant with the details of the affair and knew little about Ittoen. Therefore, contrary to our expectations, they came to have a strange sympathy with the criminal. Only a few of those in charge of proceedings sympathized with Ittoen as well as with the criminal. Newspapers described Tomita as 'a pitiful student'. The attitude of the public can be gauged by the fact that a certain mother who had been influenced by a movement of his fellow students for a reduction in his penalty, wanted to have as husband for her only daughter, 'the student who had cut his finger in expiation of his crime'.

The story became exaggerated in the telling. Headlines read: 'A Deplorable Affair at Ittoen', and it was even suggested that it was unbecoming of Ittoen to have handed over to the police a man who had not only confessed his crime but had gone so far as to cut his finger in expiation. Another

---

[1] The swastika has been a mystic symbol in the East from very ancient times. It was introduced into Europe in the sixth century A.D. When Hitler adopted it he turned its arms the opposite way.   M.B.B.

accusation was that Ittoen was guilty because it had overlooked and condoned his thefts for over a year, and so on. I know that I failed in my handling of this, but since that time many of these people have come to understand the truth.

However, there are other and more important aspects of this affair that I want to talk about. First let me quote the letter that Tomita wrote the day after he cut his finger:

'I press my palms together prayerwise before writing this letter. It was difficult to cut my finger. I tried to shirk my duty, saying, "Why must I cut it?" Then Some-One cornered me and said severely, "Yes you must". I cannot think that such a bad one as me could have a conscience or I might say that I had cornered myself. However that may be, I was certainly cornered by Some-One. I then passed several hours in a terrible, almost insane state of mind. I argued with myself, "You could deceive yourself, couldn't you?" But I couldn't do this in the presence of that Some-One. Many thoughts pursued each other through my mind . . . "Even if I did cut . . . " or "Give up! Give up!" I tried to flee this way and that, but in the end that Some-One forced me to make the decision and at once I became calm and sober. My voice chanted a short sutra. I was no longer excited. The cutting was not done in any state of excitement. However, I again attempted to conceal my crime, excusing myself because I had cut my finger in expiation. I still wanted to hide the truth or at least to cause the matter to be treated as lightly as possible. It was all in vain. I daringly called on Somekawa San and told him the truth, and yet my heart continued to cry "Conceal my crime if possible". Even after going to bed and bravely bearing the pain of the cut finger, I could not rid myself of my desire to be acquitted of my crime. Secretly I longed for some accident to happen to Somekawa San and I continued to look out for some lucky chance that would help me to escape discovery.

'Every word of your morning talk reached my heart and my breathing seemed to stifle me as I waited for the last critical moment. When you said, "The criminal has appeared", I stopped breathing altogether. Then I heard the words "It was myself" and all my evil thoughts rushed out of me with the release of my breath so that I almost fell down in the presence of everyone. Tears did not come to my eyes. Indeed, I felt neither joy nor sorrow. All my attachments, all my selfish thoughts had been cast out. Yesterday when I cut my finger at the small shrine of Fudo on the mountain behind Ittoen it was merely a physical cutting. But now it was a spiritual cutting.

'I can no longer think of concealing my crime. I can no longer tell a lie or put the blame on others. I can only confess all my sins and make a frank acknowledgement before Light. If it had not been for your last words: "It was myself", the root of my desire to conceal my sins or treat them as lightly as possible would not have been destroyed and in due course another evil sprout would have arisen from the same root.

'How shameful my attitude of fearing the worst must appear to the awakened one who regards life and death as if they were merely day and night! And how miserable does this attitude make a man like me. But now that I have confessed my crimes before Light, I am truly happy. I have nothing more to say. I can only prostrate myself to the ground, acknowledging my faults to Light and waiting for its judgement.

Dated 31.12.47.

Masaichi Tomita.'

His next letter dated 1.1.48 was written in a small room in Ittoen:

'For twenty-five years I have lived a false life in a world of evil karma. The remainder of my life must be given to penitence and must be lived in a world of expiation. Please listen to my last entreaty as if I were one of your disciples even though I may not be permitted to call myself such. Please teach me how to live for the sake of penitence and what I must do by way of expiation.'

The Power of Sange

And now ponder deeply on the tremendous power generated when all the members of Ittoen practised self-examination and were willing to take the blame for another's evil-doing. Without either blame or compulsion, the wrong-doer repented of his crime and voluntarily confessed it. His confession was something quite different from what is expected by the ordinary standards of the world and it had a tremendous effect on large numbers of people not connected with Ittoen. This is seen, for example, in the words of the public prosecutor when he remarked with genuine admiration that never before had he had experience of such a case.

Let us turn again to Tomita's letters of confession. There are several further important points in them. Take: 'You could deceive yourself, couldn't you?' and the victory of that Some-One, the conscience. And there was the state of his mind when he cut his finger without excitement and he heard his voice calmly chanting a sutra. Then in the morning worship, when he heard the words: 'The criminal has appeared' and his breathing stopped, and how, at the words, 'It was myself' all selfish thoughts left him and he almost fell down in a faint in the presence of everyone. Again, 'When I cut my finger at the small shrine of Fudo on the mountain behind Ittoen, it was merely a physical cutting. But now it was a spiritual cutting.' Finally, there is his resolution to leave the world of evil karma after having lived falsely for twenty-five years and his touching plea: 'Please listen to my last entreaty as if I were one of your disciples even though I may not be permitted to call myself such. Please teach me how to live for the sake of penitence and what I must do by way of expiation.'

When he implored me and trusted me, how could I help feeling love for him? Even if his words had been full of guile I should have been satisfied to be deceived by him in this way. And even though his own resolution might be short-lived, I could not on that account have deserted him. I have lived my life in penitence, in frank acknowledgement of my own failures and shortcomings and I have always tried not to criticize others and to trust their word.[1] Now that I had seen his finger cut in evidence of his sincerity and had heard his frank confession, I felt that it was my duty to teach him the best and highest way that I had learned through my own experience and to protect his spiritual awakening regardless of all criticism.

I sought the opinion of Mikami, the former Toban of Hoten Ittoen in Manchuria, and he thought the same as I did. Very tenderly in the presence of Mikami, Suehiro and Harakawa San I asked Tomita if he had anything more he wanted to say. He replied, 'I have one entreaty. When I have repented as fully as Ittoen will let me, may I be permitted to become a member of Ittoen again?'

I answered him, 'The door to my Roto is always open, so that you are free to come to me. But the place of your Taku-hatsu may be in prison. If you want to achieve the reality of penitence, you should make some "Friends of Penitence" in prison. Pray that you will persuade one hundred inmates there to become "Friends of Penitence".'

'I see,' he said.

I do not know how wholeheartedly he accepted my words, but I think he fixed them firmly in his mind. We were all very serious when I went on, 'You would be thinking only of yourself if you surrendered to justice merely in the expectation that your penalty would thereby be reduced. I think that you ought to hope that you will be sentenced as heavily as possible.' I said this with deep sympathy, but there were some who could not see how much I felt for him and it became the cause of misunderstanding.

In this misunderstanding we see the difference between our way of living and so-called common sense. I believe that when there is true voluntary confession there can be no thought of self and therefore I did not want him to have any hope that his sentence would be reduced. In this life of penitence we

[1] It is significant that Mahatma Gandhi always trusted another's word no matter how often he might be deceived. In the end the other person usually rose to the trust placed in him.　　　　　　　　　　　M.B.B.

expect to shoulder not merely the results of our own evil-doing but also the results of other people's. It is, however, a fact that the more one cherishes this hope of heavy punishment, the more one's punishment is reduced. Further, if one were really seeking to get one hundred 'Friends of Penitence', one's dwelling place would no longer be a prison. It would become a temple of religious self-discipline.

When people said that it was unreasonable to let Tomita deliver himself up to justice, the criticism was wholly superficial. The advice I gave him arose from my deep love for him and a thorough consideration of his case. And, I would add, this so-called 'Deplorable Affair at Ittoen' made me realize even more deeply how holy and noble is the life of Sange and it encouraged us all to practise Sange in both its material and spiritual aspects.

NOTES BY MAKOTO OHASHI

Before the trial, several members of the Judicial Committee of the House of Councillors, to which Tenko San belonged, had visited Kosenrin and one of them offered to act as counsel for the accused. Another said that the case showed the ideal solution for all administrative and criminal problems. Tenko San concluded the article from which the above is quoted, with the words, 'I pray that there may be established within the Cabinet a Sange or Penitence Ministry whose members will live according to the idea of Sange and thereby aim at a basic reform of all things pertaining to the actual life of people.'

Tomita was sentenced to three years' imprisonment and released on five years' probation. After his release he came to Tenko San who was staying outside Kosenrin and reported that he had been reinstated in college, and given financial help. He said he intended to take advantage of this and continue his medical studies. Tenko San later told us that he had prayed anxiously that Tomita should not forget the lesson of penitence and the resolution he had made when he cut his finger at the Fudo shrine.

Appendix

BEING A
DISCIPLE'S EXPERIENCES

It was at the earnest request of Marie Beuzeville Byles and with the authority of the Toban that I wrote the foregoing translation and the following story.

It is only fair to the reader to point out that it was with some reluctance that I did these things. I took up the study of English again when I was sixty years of age and after an interval of forty years. I am therefore indebted to Marie Beuzeville Byles who transcribed my manuscript from my dictionary-English and put it into idiomatic-English for Westerners . . .

When I was at the College at Kyoto it happened that there was a revolt among the students against the newly appointed president. This College was and still is the objective of aspiring young people because it has been the Alma Mater of many who distinguished themselves in after life, including some extreme leftists. The cause of the students' revolt was the new president's plan to deprive them of their freedom. They held rallies and tried to organize a strike.

Even then I had doubts as to the meaning of freedom and could not entirely agree with my fellows. At one of these meetings, when everyone was highly excited, I found myself on the platform saying, 'Friends, you shout loudly about freedom, but what is this freedom you so eagerly seek? Is it so miserable and precarious a thing that you must protect it so ardently and become fearful lest a mere new president should be able to deprive you of it?' Abruptly the hall became quiet, and I went on, 'I think that a man who is truly free will never lose his freedom even though he be within prison walls. What do you think about that?' The dead silence continued as I stepped down from the platform.

The revolt resulted in a victory for the students, some of whom later became cabinet ministers, leaders of political parties, managers of large business firms, and noted journalists. But for me that question, 'What is true freedom?' became an omen for my future life. To find its answer was the first of the three reasons that ultimately drove me to Tenko San and Ittoen.

After I left college, I engaged in contracting work. Then when I was thirty years old I read Tenko San's *Life of Sange*. It impressed me tremendously, and reading this as well as other of Tenko San's writings was the second thing that brought me to Ittoen. What impressed me most was his firm faith that one can live without possessing a penny, that such a life is utterly worth living and wholly satisfying, that it was the life lived by the spiritual teachers of old, and finally that it could be followed equally well by educated and uneducated, rich and poor, young and old, healthy and invalid, men and women. I thought to myself that if I could live such a miraculous life for even one day, I would be content to die the day after. At that time I could not live without money for a single minute, and I desired money very much even though it sometimes caused me distress.

The third reason I came to Ittoen is one about which I am reluctant to speak. When I was young I had secretly fallen in love with a teenage Geisha girl from the north country. She was so skilled at dancing, singing and other arts that she was a first favourite in the gay quarter of the town, but nonetheless she was determined to keep her life pure until the time of her formal marriage, and to do this despite the somewhat loose-living atmosphere of her environment, with a result

171

that she was called *Otoko-killai* (a woman who hates men). That she was the heiress of the owner of a large restaurant and cinema theatre made her financially independent, so that she was able to keep to her determination more easily. She seemed far too high above me for marriage, and in due course I was married to another.

A few years later I occasionally met the Geisha girl at dinner parties[1] and found that she had been secretly in love with me all the time. Then the tragedy began. My wife was tender and true to me, and I tried, of course in vain, to love both women at the same time. I knew I should give up this illicit love. But the root of my wrong-doing lay far deeper and misled me, not only in this matter but in my whole way of living. Up till then I had caught only a glimpse of Tenko San when I heard him lecture, but reading his books made me realize the basic cause of my error and showed me that I could root it out only by *dying to self*. I realized that this alone could prevent the ruin of all three of us.

I asked my wife if she would come with me to Ittoen, but she did not have good health and felt that the austerity of Ittoen life would be beyond her capacity. I also parted from the Geisha girl and abandoned my family. Later on my father came to understand why I did this terrible thing.

I went straight to Ittoen and Tenko San, seeking guidance to Truth and a right way of living.

Tenko San took me outside the precincts of Kosenrin and back across the bridge by which one enters. Not until many years later did I realize that his object was to meet me on the street homeless and propertyless and in the position of Roto. Ittoen, the Garden of the One Light, is the spiritual side of the new life. Kosenrin demonstrates Senkosha, the practical, social and economic side of Ittoen's way of life when one realizes that the origin of suffering and evil lies within one's heart. The existence of Kosenrin shows that when there is this

---

[1] Of course, the Japanese wife does not attend, or at least did not then attend, dinner parties with her husband.   M.B.B.

understanding, it is possible in actual fact to live both without discord and also successfully from the economic angle.

Tenko San took me outside the protection of Kosenrin as it were and said, 'Well, what is it you want to tell me?'

As I had read several of his books and once heard him lecture, I thought I understood the theory of Ittoen's life passably well, so I thereupon started on a long harangue concerning my opinions of Ittoen. He listened in silence. After a while I began to lose my certainty. Finally I asked, 'Am I wrong?'

He replied, 'Yes, you are wrong.' He paused and then pointing down the road, added 'Go down this way to the hut over there called Hatake-no-koya, eat there and stay the night.' Hatake-no-koya was only two or three hundred metres from Kosenrin, but it was run as a separate unit. It gave to all who came two meals and one night's lodging, and the opportunity of finding a new way of life.

Tenko San went back to Kosenrin. I stood a short while undecided. I was very dissatisfied with his reception. But I had wagered my life or death on Ittoen, and I knew I could not withdraw until I had found out whether Tenko San was a saint or a hypocrite. I was desperately determined on this quest for truth. At length I went down to the hut Hataka-no-koya. It was a small hut, the food was so poor I could scarcely swallow a mouthful, and the space too crowded for the men there to stretch out properly on the floor to sleep. The railway line lay close to it, and whenever a train passed, the ground rumbled and the hut shook. It was the most miserable night I had ever spent.

In the morning Tenko San sent a message for me to come over to his small room in Kosenrin.

'How was it?' he asked.

I answered, 'I suppose Ittoen's way of life may show me the path to Truth by forcing me to practise Geza to the uttermost limit.' Geza literally means to prostrate on the ground but it also means to do the humblest work and to place oneself in the most inferior position both formally and spiritually.

Tenko San replied softly, 'Perhaps that may be so.' His face had a gentleness quite different from the grimness I had seen on it the day before. He went on, 'Now that you have eaten and slept in that hut, I want to prevent you from taking a wrong course even by a single step.'

Since then I have lived a new life for close on thirty years. But not until ten years later did I realize that it was then that I was saved—fed by Light or Fukuden. To die to self is easy to talk about and understand intellectually, but to live it as a reality was far from easy. It has been the one great Koan during all those thirty years of Ittoen life.

About five years after starting this new life, Tenko San suddenly said to me, 'What would you think about marrying Miss C?' Miss C. was another member of Ittoen.

I replied, 'My mind has become as if I had given an all-inclusive power of attorney, especially concerning the matter of marriage. I have no longer any desire or will of my own.' My answer was the culmination of a long meditation on that Koan 'to die to self' which had filled my whole mind during the hours of doing Takuhatsu and living the lowliest life of Roto.

Tenko San then said, 'If that is the case I'll say, please get married.' I knew I must take this as a request of Light. Tenko San continued, 'But perhaps I should first ask you a second and rather important question. Do you think you could get along all right with Miss C?'

I answered, 'At least I know I am a man with many faults.' He nodded. We were duly married, in obedience to Tenko San's order. Now I have a daughter who is a teacher and herself married to a member of Ittoen; they have a child and this makes me a grandfather. I have also a son who is attending the same university college as I was attending forty-seven years ago.

About a year after my second marriage, the Geisha girl herself came to Ittoen from a long way, and zealously practised

Takuhatsu for five years. Then she was called back to inherit her parents' property, and Tenko San agreed that she should go. I hear that she is still unmarried and is now the managing director of the restaurant and the cinema theatre. I have had no news of my first wife, but I ceaselessly ask her forgiveness. I know that I am open to every reproach, but nonetheless I think that from the very beginning I was destined to come to Ittoen.

At the commencement of my new Ittoen life I was given Takuhatsu in the form of kitchen work, wood-chopping, bath preparation, making brooms from twigs and selling them in the town, farming, type-picking and setting, proof-reading of books and periodicals published in Kosenrin, and at one time I went in the position of Roto to do Takuhatsu in the centre of Tokyo. At other times I went to render some specific service in the outside world.

The last type of service included a sojourn in Nagoya, the third largest city in Japan. There was then an enormous number of unemployed living on government relief; the Department of Home Affairs therefore instituted training centres in the six largest cities, and called for officers to take charge of the training courses with a view to enabling such as would to start a new life. There was considerable difficulty in getting the necessary officers. I was the head of the four requested by Ittoen to undertake this work. The results were good and many provincial papers remarked on our success. We were treated well and given good salaries which of course we dedicated to Light and Kosenrin, and, as always, worked without payment for ourselves. Perhaps I should also mention that, at a later date when I inherited my father's property, this too was given to Light.

When I was something over fifty years old a new sort of Takuhatsu was allotted to me. The headmaster of Ittoen's school asked me to teach mathematics. Although I had up to a point specialized in mathematics when I was at the College and had liked the subject well enough, nonetheless I had no confidence in my ability to teach, more especially as it was over thirty years since I had given up my studies. However, although there are no rules at Ittoen, it is basic that a member has no business of his own because he has died to self, and must therefore do whatever anyone, especially a Toban, asks him to do. On account of my having completed the junior examination at the College, in due course the educational authorities gave me the prescribed licence to teach. The classes are still small, for the total number of Ittoen members is under 400. The usual number in a class is between four and ten.

In the course of my teaching, I lost all my teeth. As it is a principle of Ittoen life that we should live as frugally as possible, I hesitated to ask the Toban if I might obtain artificial dentures. However, eventually I did so and they made it easier for the children to understand my teaching. Also they made it possible for me to learn English and so help in what to me is the holy work of translating Tenko San's writings.

As to the true freedom about which I had spoken to the College students, and which was my first reason for coming to Ittoen, I have found, not through meditation but through experience, that my freedom is curtailed only by my own selfish desires, and that non-possession, both material and spiritual, is the free way of life.

Although my Congregationalist uncle failed to impress me with Christianity in my boyhood, I have since heard about the Gospels and found myself strongly drawn towards Jesus Christ. I feel very close to the breathing of Christ during his last moments on the Cross. It stirs me more than many lectures or sermons. I picture him killed on the Cross, all alone, surrounded by scornful and contemptuous people. Very few, I think, appreciate the bliss he must have experienced when all were against him. Only those who have themselves been beset by adversaries and borne the situation as he did, can understand the bliss of utter loneliness.

I think I know from actual experience that Ittoen life ought to be a series of small crosses, in bearing which, there is joy.

Tenko San once said, 'Not every man can be a Carnegie, but everyone can be a Christ.'

Tenko San's new life originated precisely because of his consciousness of his own inadequacy and wrong-doing. Sange would not be necessary for the man who is always right. He says that every act and every breathing must be an expression of Sange, constant mindfulness of one's inadequacy.

Trifling as one's life may seem, if it is to be worth living it must be fundamentally helpful for solution of all difficulties, not only one's own but also those of the whole world. Tenko San's new life during its sixty years was beset by so many realities that it is a living example. My above story is only the poor experience of a foolish man who has blindly followed Tenko San through his life. It shows only a small part of Ittoen life whose essence is deep, broad, complex and many-sided, so I conclude my story by quoting Marie Byles' words:

'The more I ponder over the term Sange in the light of the stories and admonitions of Tenko San, the more I am satisfied that its overtone is that of dissipation of egoism, an overtone not conveyed by the English words penitence or repentance. Individual selfness lies at the core of all evil and is the root of all evil. With this in mind we can understand how one's very breathing should be an expression of Sange, not remorse for our shortcomings which only brings despair, but a mindfulness that our egoism is separating us from the Great Oneness and preventing peace both inner and outer.

And thus we come back to the age-old truth that lies at the heart of all religions. Tenko San has thrown a startling new light on this truth by showing the need of the individual to accept the responsibility for all evil. But the need for self-naughting or dying to self has been known for thousands of years. It is the one great Koan that all truth-seekers have tried to answer.'

M. Ohashi

For those who wish to
communicate with Ittoen,
write:
C/o Ittoen,
Yamashina,
Kyoto, Japan

Glossary

AMITA or AMIDA

The Buddha of Boundless Light, vowed to save all people who put their trust in him. The Saint Honen, the teacher of Shinran mentioned in the text, taught that all that was necessary for salvation was the ceaseless repetition with faith of the name of the Buddha Amita.

BODHIDHARMA

The sage who brought Zen Buddhism to China in the sixth century A.D.

BODHISATTVA

A perfected one who renounces Nirvana and returns to earth to help all sentient beings attain Buddhahood.

BUDDHA SAKYAMUNI

The historical Buddha, Gautama, born in Nepal in the sixth century B.C.

BUDDHA AMITA

See Amita.

BUDDHISM

Tenko San always refers to Mahayana Buddhism, the Buddhism of the northern countries, which differs widely from Theravada or Hinayana Buddhism of Southern Asia. Both claim to stem from the Buddha Sakyamuni's teaching.

FUKUDEN

Selfless or purified wealth. A man's spiritual and material wealth are changed to Fukuden when he realizes that a life of non-possession which outwardly appears precarious is in fact the most solid and stable. Fukuden is the joy and peace that a person finds within his heart when, in consequence of this understanding, he begins to give up acquisitiveness and greed. Material things, too, become Fukuden when those things that are necessary are given to the one who needs them. But if one expends material things wrongfully one can never find Fukuden. Therefore Fukuden is both a purified heart and purified material things.

GEISHA GIRL

Geisha girls are not prostitutes. They come of good family and must naturally be talented as well as good-looking. They are highly trained in various arts such as flower arrangement, tea ceremony, dancing and music. They must also be adept at entertaining and handling men. When fully trained a Geisha girl usually finds a patron, generally a wealthy business man, and becomes his mistress exclusively. She earns high wages and only the wealthy can afford a Geisha party. The Geisha girl provides the cultured feminine companionship not expected of a wife who never accompanies her husband to parties (except perhaps in a very Westernized family).

GEZA

Literally to prostrate on the ground—to take the lowliest position possible, mentally as well as physically.

GODDESS OF MERCY

Kwannon.

GURU

The Indian name for a spiritual teacher.

HUNGRY GHOSTS

Popular Buddhism believes that people are reborn in various forms, among these are the pretas or hungry ghosts. These are depicted as having huge bellies craving to be filled, and pin-sized mouths incapable of taking food. They are the ghosts of people who as human beings were always grasping for more and more. Ceremonies for hungry ghosts are very common in Japan.

ITTOEN

The Garden or Compound of the One Light. Ittoen is a way of life which follows from rebirth into the world of Light, the Kingdom of God or the Buddha world, or another level of consciousness. Conversion, Satori, and Entering the Stream are other expressions for the entrance into this new life as Tenko San calls it. The essence of this new life is a reorientation away from self towards Light (or Christ). Tenko San speaks of it as dying to self. The

Ittoen way of life that follows is based upon Sange (see later) and humble service.

JIZO

The guardian deity of a family.

KARMA

The law of action, that we reap what we have sown, either in this life or in another.

KOAN

A kind of nonsense riddle, the constant meditation upon which is used by the Rinzai sect of Zen Buddhism to overthrow the intellect and reveal a wisdom beyond intellect.

KOYUKAI

Friends of Light—the Society of lay disciples of Ittoen.

LIGHT

Tenko San's term for God. That which Alone Is, the One Reality.

MAHAYANA BUDDHISM

The Buddhism of the northern countries of Asia including Japan. It is the Greater Vehicle, in contrast to the Hinayana or Smaller Vehicle, the Greater because it aspired to take all to Nirvana, and lay people as well as monks and nuns.

O BENJO

Honourable toilet.

ROKUMAN-GYOGAN

The prayer that our humble service may be accepted by Light—see translation in Introduction. The name was coined by Tenko San. 'Roku' means six, the six paths of Zen to reach the Further Shore or Enlightenment, namely alms-giving, keeping the Precepts, perseverance, hard training, equanimity, attainment of wisdom. 'Man' means 10,000. Tenko San aspired to visit five homes for toilet cleaning each day he went out and to go out 200 days in the year, that is 1,000 per annum or 10,000 in ten years. 'Gyogan' means a prayer.

ROTO

The state of a beggar, homeless and penniless, living on the streets. As originally used by Tenko San, the term did mean this, for members of Ittoen in the beginning had no home at all. Even today they are expected to be so completely trustful of Light that they must be able to return to this homeless state at any time. But also, for Ittoen, Roto is the spiritual state of one not attached to knowledge, self-pride, worldly love, and not resentful of suffering or unpleasant mental states. This non-attachment is true freedom, spiritually, as homelessness is true freedom physically.

SAKYAMUNI
See BUDDHA.

SANGE
Literally penitence or repentance. For Tenko San it means taking upon oneself the responsibility for all the evils of the world, that is to say, never blaming anyone other than oneself. Giving up self-righteousness perhaps explains it most easily. If one waits for the other person to admit that he is wrong, the discord will seldom be healed. But if one takes all the blame oneself, the discord is healed at once. Tenko San considers that this is the only path to personal, social and world peace. But to be effective it must be accompanied by humble selfless services rendered to Light. The term also carries the idea of renunciation of self not carried by the English words penitence or repentance.

SENKOSHA
The practical, social, economic and business side of life when one moves with Formless Light and in the spirit of penitence and humble selfless service.

SHINRAN (1173-1263)
The disciple of Honen, who taught that dependence on the grace of the Buddha Amita and ceaseless repetition of his name were alone necessary for salvation. Shinran broke with the tradition that marriage for a priest was not the ideal. He himself discarded his monastic robes and shaven head, and lived an ordinary householder's life. He carried his master's doctrine of salvation by faith to greater extremes, and became the founder of the branch of Jodo (or Pure Land) Buddhism known as Shinshu.

SHUGYO
It originates from Buddhism and it has two sides. One is a way of self-discipline, aiming at the elevation of one's character, or deliverance of one's soul, or achievement of one's spiritual awakening (or enlightenment). Sakyamuni's meditation for many years

for the purpose of finding a solution of all problems in human life is a sort of Shugyo. Bodhidharma performed Shugyo by sitting against the wall for nine years. In this meaning there are many ways and means of Shugyo. The other side is a way of saving people in misery and contributing to the peace of the world. Rokuman Gyogan of Ittoen is also a sort of Shugyo.

SUTRA

A sacred chant, or a Buddhist scripture.

TAKUHATSU

Literally means to get one's food in everyday life. In common usage it refers to the practice of Buddhist monks and nuns going begging. They take the bowl or bag and receive what food or money is offered by various homes. In Ittoen's sense Takuhatsu means humble selfless service rendered without expectation of reward or thanks, but only as an offering to Light out of gratitude for the opportunity of being able to help expiate the evils of the world. Behind both uses of the term is the idea of complete dependence upon Light (or God or Buddha).

TEA HOUSE

This serves many purposes. It is a restaurant, night club and hotel combined. Clients of the upper classes come to eat, drink, be entertained by Geisha girls, or stay the night.

TOBAN

A director in charge of some department of Ittoen's affairs in its community life.

ZAZEN

Meditation.

ZEN

The sect of Mahayana Buddhism best known in the West. Daito-kuji mentioned in the text is one of the headquarters of Zen in Japan.

ZENDO

Meditation hall.